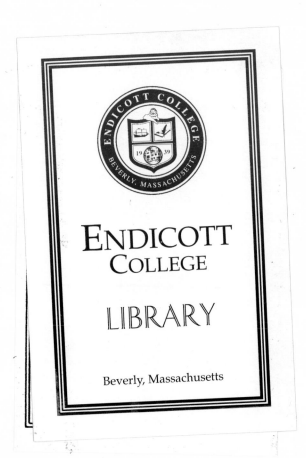

ENDICOTT
COLLEGE

LIBRARY

Beverly, Massachusetts

POSTPARTUM DEPRESSION

GARLAND REFERENCE LIBRARY
OF SOCIAL SCIENCE
(VOL. 335)

POSTPARTUM DEPRESSION

GARLAND REFERENCE LIBRARY
OF SOCIAL SCIENCE
(VOL. 335)

POSTPARTUM DEPRESSION
A Research Guide and
International Bibliography

Laurence Kruckman
Chris Asmann-Finch

GARLAND PUBLISHING, INC. • NEW YORK & LONDON
1986

Library of Congress Cataloging-in-Publication Data
Kruckman, Laurence, 1943–
  Postpartum depression.

  (Garland reference library of social science;
vol. 335)
  Includes indexes.
  1. Postpartum psychiatric disorders—Abstracts.
1. Asmann-Finch, Chris. II. Title. III. Series:
Garland reference library of social science; v. 335.
[DNLM: 1. Depression—abstracts. 2. Depressive Disorders—
abstracts. 3. Psychotic Disorders—abstracts.
4. Puerperal Disorders—abstracts. ZWQ 500 K94p]
RG850.K78 1986   016.61685'27   85-31136
ISBN 0-8240-9121-3 (alk. paper)

Printed on acid-free, 250-year-life paper
Manufactured in the United States of America

To
Verna Irene Asmann
and
Mary Stewart

CONTENTS

ACKNOWLEDGMENTS

This research was partially funded by the National Institute of Mental Health, a post-doctoral fellowship at the University of Illinois Medical Center, School of Public Health, and a grant from The Graduate School, Indiana University of Pennsylvania. Much of the introduction was co-authored with Gwen Stern, Department of Anthropology, Northwestern University, and appeared in SOCIAL SCIENCE AND MEDICINE 17:1027-41, 1983. The bibliography was compiled with the assistance of June Craig, Sharon Svennsen, and Alvin Cox. Further selections and annotations were completed by Carolyn White, Ann Blatherwick, and Indiana University of Pennsylvania students Brenda Ferguson and Margaret Augustyn. Parts of the manuscript were typed by Sharon Richwine, and the word processing and programming were done by Chris Asmann-Finch and Jennifer and Jeff Moore. Early drafts of the project were reviewed by Susan M. Ford, Department of Anthropology, Southern Illinois University. Additional assistance was provided by Coleen Seagren, The Graduate School, Bill Creighton, Information Systems, Indiana University, the Frontier Nursing Service, School of Midwifery and Family Nursing, and Carolyn Tilley, National Library of Medicine, Bethesda, Maryland.

PREFACE

The transitory postpartum "blues" affect from 50 to 80% of mothers in the Western world. Fortunately it is self-limiting and symptoms subside within 3 days. However, the symptoms for moderate postpartum depression are much more serious and affect 3 to 20% of all new mothers. The symptoms may last from a few weeks to several months; 4% of the cases persist for as long as a year.

Depression is not the only negative reaction to childbirth; the postpartum period is also linked to mother-infant bonding problems, child abuse, marital difficulties and divorce, and suicide. Besides the obvious personal pain of adjustment, the long term societal effects are immense.

Unfortunately most literature regarding etiology and treatment falls into two camps: the biogenic and psychogenic. Rarely do the disciplines cross lines. The goal of this review is to bring together research from diverse disciplines and journals in hopes of stimulating new perspectives.

Western reductionist research has provided many gifts. However, in the case of postpartum depression, isolated, narrow research has not provided the necessary answers regarding cause or treatment. We hope this resource will encourage multi-disciplinary research that includes social as well as biological variables and that examines the variables in wider social contexts such as the family. Suggestions and comments would be appreciated by the authors: please write, Laurence Kruckman, Ph.D., Department of Sociology-Anthropology, Indiana University of Pennsylvania, Indiana, Pennsylvania, 15705.

INTRODUCTION

I. INTRODUCTION TO POSTPARTUM RESEARCH

One clearly negative outcome of the perinatal period is the occurrence of postpartum depression. However, the nature of this phenomenon--as a disease and as an illness--remains unclear. The very term used to describe this disease syndrome--"depression" has deep experiential and emotional connotations in Western culture. The term "postpartum depression" has been applied rather imprecisely to include both mild, transient forms of depression which are quite common in the first postpartum days, as well as to the more severe psychotic reactions which are quite rare. Typically, the syndrome is characterized by feelings of sadness in the new mother, heightened emotional lability, weeping, irritability, and fatigue. This lack of precision has resulted in confusion in distinguishing discrete behavioral manifestations from behaviors which may constitute a clinical psychiatric entity (c.f. Frate et al., 1979 [190]).

While there is great interest in the shorter, more transient form of postpartum depression--commonly referred to as "baby blues" or postpartum "blues"--in the popular culture as reflected in articles in women's magazines as well as "folk" knowledge (e.g., Gazella, 1981 [205]), the medical and psychiatric literature reflects a preoccupation with the more severe postpartum psychosis. As Yalom et al., note: "The transient mild depression occurring postpartum (the "postpartum blues") is so ubiquitous and ostensibly benign that it has not often been deemed worthy of serious study" (1968:16 [655]). Even less well studied or defined is a phenomenon which some researchers view as intermediate to postpartum baby blues and psychosis in terms of its duration and severity and which may represent a separate clinical entity of postpartum depression (Paykel, 1980 [476]).

Much of the research on postpartum depression has looked to biological and/or psychosocial factors in etiology such as: hormonal shifts, maternal age and parity, psychiatric history, marital relationship, etc. Little attention has been given to consideration of the impact of the cultural patterning of the postpartum period--e.g., the structure, organization of the family and social group, role expectations of the new mother and significant others, etc.--on the etiology and manifestation of postpartum depression. Research literature suggests that milder forms of postpartum depression, including the so-called "baby blues" may represent a continuum of physiological processes, and that the behavioral manifestation and even the subjective emotional experience of "depression" can be exacerbated or muted by sociocultural factors (Stern & Kruckman, 1983 [584]).

Interestingly, a review of the anthropological literature reveals surprisingly little evidence of the phenomenon identified in Western psychiatric and popular diagnoses as postpartum depression.

In the following review, postpartum depression is examined as a context in which to analyze the interaction between biological and sociocultural processes. This introductory essay begins with a review of explanations and approaches to etiology in the medical, psychological and anthropological literature, followed by an examination of the crosscultural literature on childbirth which suggests that there are some common elements in the social structuring of the postpartum period cross-culturally which may prevent postpartum depression.

II. THE PHENOMENON OF POSTPARTUM DEPRESSION

A. Definitions

In this introduction postpartum depression will be defined using the following three-part categorization adapted from Brown (1979 [94]) and others:

1. <u>Postpartum psychosis</u> or puerperal psychosis--a relatively rare disorder that usually occurs in the first three months, particularly the first two weeks, following childbirth with symptoms similar to general psychotic

reactions: confusion, fatigue, agitation, alterations in mood, feelings of hopelessness and shame, delusions or auditory hallucinations, hyperactivity, and rapid speech or mania.

2. Chronic depressive syndrome or moderate depression disorder--more debilitating than the "blues" and more common than postpartum psychotic reactions, this still poorly defined syndrome is characterized by despondency, tearfulness, feelings of inadequacy, guilt, anxiety, irritability, and fatigue. Symptoms occur in early months of the postpartum and can persist for more than a year. Researchers suggest that women experiencing this form of depression rarely seek treatment, are almost never hospitalized, and only recently are being studied.

3. Postpartum "blues" or transitory minor affective disorder--the name most commonly used to describe the weeping and emotional lability that occur during the first postpartum week. Descriptions of symptoms include frequent and prolonged crying, irritability, poor sleep, mood changes, and a sense of vulnerability that may continue for several weeks. Onset is within three days following childbirth.

B. Incidence

While the above description of postpartum reactions at first glance appears precise, the "condition" is a complex melange of physical, emotional, and behavioral changes. Attempts to study the incidence of postpartum depression have suffered, too, from the problems plaguing most psychosocial epidemiology: 1) divergent diagnostic criteria, and 2) biased samples due to inconsistent referrals. As a result, many researchers have suggested caution in interpreting the results of the clinical studies which represent the vast majority of postpartum research.

Postpartum psychosis is reported to be a relatively rare disorder occurring in an average of 1 per 1,000 births. Onset is acute, usually within the first three months: 80 percent of all cases are present within 3-14 days after a symptom-free period. It is interesting to note that the incidence rates of postpartum psychosis have remained unchanged since the 1850s and that studies in various settings have produced similar estimates of rate. Even if we assume variations through time in diagnostic criteria and recording techniques, the above studies tend to indicate stable rates for 130 years regarding postpartum psychosis.

The incidence for moderate depression is much more variable, ranging from 30 to 200 cases per 1,000 births (see Table 1). Depression may occur at any time after delivery, often after the woman has returned home from the hospital. The symptoms may last from a few weeks to several months; about 4 percent of the cases persist for as long as a year (Gelder, 1978:88 [206]).

Transitory "blues," like the more debilitating postpartum psychosis, has a quick onset, usually 1-3 days postpartum. Incidence rates range from 500 to 800 cases per 1,000 births depending on diagnostic criteria, time and location of the study (see Table 1).

C. Historical Perspectives

Postpartum emotional problems, especially psychosis, were one of the few clearly recognized psychiatric entities during the 19th century. No doubt this awareness reflected the much earlier writings of Hippocrates, who in 700 B.C. described the emotional problems of the postpartum woman in detail, as well as the writings of Galen, Celsus, and others. By 1858, Marce had published a definitive study, Traits de la folie des femmes enceintes [387], linking negative emotional reactions with childbirth.

The history of postpartum psychosis treatment after 1860, however, illustrates the power of diagnostic criteria to affect attitudes and research foci. By the late 19th century, Kraepelinian criteria were in effect and did not include a category for postpartum depression. Some afflicted women, it seemed, belonged to the "manic depressive" universe, others "dementia praecox," still others "toxic confusion" or "neurotic states." As a result, many early psychiatrists concluded, as had Kraepelin, that "postpartum psychosis" did not exist as a separate syndrome (Brockington et al., 1978:49 [89]). By 1940 Jacobs stated that "every reaction type may occur during the puerperium," hence, "puerperal psychosis as a clinical entity does not exist" (1943:246 [285]). Foundeur et al. were even more emphatic: "the results would not appear to justify terming the postpartum illness as a separate illness any more than one might term those young patients who react unfavorably to college as sufferers from a 'college psychosis'" (1957:509 [188]).

As early as 1920, registries, including the International Nomenclature of Disease, removed this diagnostic entity, which effectively restricted the gathering of data on it as a separate phenomenon.

This skepticism about postpartum depression as a clinical entity continues today. The Diagnostic and Statistical Manual (DSM) II (1968) described a separate entity: "294.4 Psychosis with Childbirth," but DSM III (1980) eliminated this category stating: "there is no compelling evidence that postpartum psychosis is a distinct entity" (1980:373). Instead, readers are referred to differential diagnoses, including schizophrenia, schizophreniform disorder, brief reactive psychosis, atypical psychosis, manic episode, major depressive episode, delirium, etc.

D. Etiology

1. Biological Theories

The psychopharmacology revolution was in full swing by 1955, and it stimulated a renewed interest in the relationship between postpartum depression and hormonal changes. It has been consistently noted that onset of symptoms on the third day postpartum corresponds strikingly to third day postpartum hormonal changes, leading to investigations of hormonal involvement in postpartum depression. Two research approaches have been taken. First, hormonal events unique to the postpartum period were examined, and data from depressed and nondepressed postpartum women were compared. Second, those physiological findings correlated with depression in general were examined in postpartum women to ascertain if the mechanisms or processes were similar or unique in the postpartum period.

One striking and well-researched hormonal change during the postpartum period is the precipitous fall in estrogen and progesterone. Estrogen and progesterone, the female reproductive hormones, increased tenfold during pregnancy (Hytten & Leitch, 1969 [280]) through the primary mechanism of synthesis by the fetoplacental unit (Goddin & Chance, 1976 [211]). Once the placenta is removed after parturition, the drop in estrogen and progesterone to prepregnant levels is sharp and immediate. By three days postpartum, estrogen and progesterone are near prepregnant levels (Hytten & Leitch, 1964). Nott et al. (1976 [450]) concluded after examining the hormone levels of 27 women before and after delivery that women with the greatest drop in progesterone levels after delivery were more likely to rate themselves depressed within ten days of delivery. Handley et al. (1977 [246]), Livingston (1978 [364]) and Stein et al. (1976 [580]) note a relationship between a rapid drop in estrogen levels at childbirth and a decrease in free plasmatryptophan levels to be correlated with depression.

A more recent research focus has been in the area of prolactin activity during the puerperium. Prolactin levels form a reverse curve of the estrogen and progesterone levels during the postpartum period, with low levels occurring immediately after parturition and increasing to a high level plateau by the first week postpartum. In additional research on hospitalization prior to surgery, prolactin has been found to increase during episodes of emotional or physical stress.

Adrenal steroid changes noted in the puerperium and possibly related to depression are: 1) changes in plasma cortisol which regulates the metabolism of fats, carbohydrates and protein; 2) an increase in aldosterone which results in an increased sodium and water retention and concomitant decrease in potassium concentration; and 3) changes in glucose tolerance with a tendency toward hypoglycemia (a change noted in depression in general). The role of cyclic adenosine monophosphate (AMP) in the transmission of nerve impulses has been linked to postpartum depression in some research based on assumptions concerning the deficiency of monoamine in the synaptic cleft. Ballinger et al. (1979 [36]) noted that cyclic AMP is elevated during the puerperium compared to two to three months postpartum. They determined that women who experienced the most mood changes had large increases in cyclic AMP during the puerperium. Yalom et al. (1968 [655]) suggested that cyclic AMP might also be a key to the frequently noted relationship between a long, difficult labor and subsequent depression.

Although hormonal research has identified potential links with depression--estrogen, progesterone, corticosteroids, and cyclic AMP--much of the research has been problematic. For example, various diurnal hormonal changes/rhythms occur in late pregnancy, making research difficult. Also, there is a general lack of knowledge concerning individual variations in hormonal levels, the importance of hormonal synchrony, and the ability of individuals to adapt to changes.

Another difficulty with this research is that the primary focus has been on psychotic reactions; researchers have ignored hormonal studies on the larger phenomenon of the "blues" or moderate depression disorders. As a result of utilizing psychotic patients, the sample sizes have been small and the focus has been on individuals.

Asch and Rubin suggest that perhaps previous research has been measuring effect rather than cause based on their observations of depression in new fathers and grandmothers: "...postpartum reactions in many cases are primarily psychogenic since the reactions occur in individuals who are not physiologically involved" (1974:874 [18]).

Since psychological stimuli affect the neuroendocrine systems, hormonal studies must be carried out in connection with psychosocial research. In an article reviewing the hormonal link to postpartum depression, Gelder states: "...the balance of evidence points to social and psychological causes for these states" (1978:89 [206]).

> it is...clear that we have not yet reached
> the point when even the first stage of
> research is likely to yield useful answers.
> Before we come back to it, there is much to
> be done in adding to knowledge of individual
> differences in endocrine readjustments after
> childbirth, and in describing in a reliable
> way the separate depressive syndromes in
> pregnancy and the puerperium. Otherwise we
> shall be guessing as wildly about hormonal
> causes of postpartum depression as did
> Prichard's generation about the circulation
> of the blood. (1978:89)

2. Psychological Variables

a. Personality Variables

Psychological factors, although difficult to separate from environmental and social context variables, are thought to play a major role in postpartum depression. In many of the studies a major complaint reported by the new mothers was a feeling of "inadequacy" regarding childrearing. Tentoni and High (1980 [600]) have suggested that postpartum depression is in part related to the explicitness of role expectations of motherhood and the female role--roles that have changed dramatically in the past 50 years. In other research, role conflict has been identified as an important social variable predictive of emotional problems (c.f. Brown and Shereshefsky, 1972 [95]; Yalom et al., 1968 [655]; Markham, 1961 [388]; Melges, 1968 [406].

Closely related to notions of role conflict is the frequent finding that "attitude" towards pregnancy, especially ambivalence, is a strong correlate of depression (Nilsson and Almgren, 1970:92 [441]; Kumer and Robson, 1978 [341]). "Sexual identity," another concept related to notions of role, has also been suggested as offering clues

xx

to the development of psychological symptoms following childbirth (Brown and Shereshefksy, 1972:139 [95]). Specifically, Nilsson and Almgren (1970:95 [441]) found women who assessed themselves more "masculine" than others reported fewer psychiatric symptoms during pregnancy but more during the postpartum. They found that "masculine" women less often stated that their husbands or boyfriends were the dominant partner in their relationship. They also reported poor contact with their mothers during childhood. The authors interpreted this to mean that the father was the major object of identification.

b. Environmental Variables

It has been hypothesized for about two centuries that broadscale social change, such as wars and economic depression, played a role in postpartum depression. In 1814, Esquirol noted an increase in postpartum depression during the invasion of France and the fall of Napoleon; Karnish and Hope identified a similar increase in the U.S. during the 1930-35 economic depression (Cruickshank, 1940 [142]); Vislie noted these increases in Norway during World War II (Seager, 1960:227 [599]). In the 1930s, Wick states that marital difficulties related to societal stress were a key to postpartum depression in over 30 percent of recorded cases (1941:299 [647]).

Several researchers tested variables associated with environmental conditions such as financial stress, socioeconomic status (SES), geographic mobility, etc. Uddenberg et al., in a study of 95 Swedish women attending prenatal clinics, noted a relationship between SES or "poor social condition" and postpartum depression (1975:160 [615]). The lower the "social condition" the higher the chances for depression.

Heitler (1976 [264]) was more specific and tied depression to pregnant or recent mothers' worries over financial matters and concern regarding the reliability of their mates' employment situation. Gordon and Gordon identified recent family "economic shifts" as a factor in a new mother's emotional adjustment (1967:359 [217]).

xxi

Davidson (1972 [156]), in his study of Jamaican women, observed an association between depression and low SES, but suggested that the real factors were a combination of low SES, large family size, and major responsibility for family support.

Concerning housing conditions and residential permanence, in a study of 120 women attending postnatal clinics in London, Paykel et al. (1980 [476]) detected an interrelationship with moderate depression and "housing quality." Nilsson and Almgren (1970 [441]) found similar results. Heitler (1976 [264]), in a study of 91 U.S. mothers, determined geographic mobility to be important as well; Gordon and Gordon (1967 [217]) concur and specify an unexpected or recent move as a key. In related research Kendel et al. found a correlation between "psychiatric mortality" and recent immigration to England (1976:297 [323]).

c. Interpersonal Variables

Interpersonal factors such as family interaction, companionship, and marital problems have also been suggested as important factors in postpartum depression. Douglas (1963 [171]), Heitler (1976 [264]), and Uddenber (1975 [615]) isolated "mother-daughter interaction" as an important variable, although detailed descriptions vary. Uddenberg found a correlation between "repudiation of mother" and depression (1975:164 [615]), while Heitler describes similar results when a "hostile" attitude exists between mother and daughter (1970 [441]). Also, Uddenberg (1975 [615]) found lack of meaningful support via family or friends related to depression, and it may be that lack of support is also linked to mother-daughter interaction.

An interrelationship between mother-infant bonding problems and subsequent postpartum depression has been suggested (Bensel and Paxson, 1977 [49]; Kitzinger, 1975 [328]). Marital problems before and after childbirth have been correlated with depression by several researchers (Heitler, 1976 [264]; Robson and Kumer, 1980 [517]; Nilsson and Almgren, 1970 [441]). Gordon and Gordon (1967 [217]) felt the probability of depression was increased if marriage partners differed in age and religion. Paykel et al. (1980 [476]), however, found "marital tension" an important factor only if other stressful life events were present.

d.   Other Variables

Kendell et al. (1976 [323]) correlated age with depression: either young or old primiparous mothers appear to be most vulnerable. Uddenberg et al. (1975 [615]) claim any mother under the age of 23 is a strong candidate for depression, while Stahlie (1960 [579]) found this to be true only for mothers 16-17 years of age. Yalom et al. (1968 [655]) concluded that age of first menses correlated more strongly with depression than age at first pregnancy.

Parity is also suggested frequently as an associated factor. Davidson (1972 [156]), Yalom et al. (1968 [755]), Kendell et al. (1976 [323]), and Jackson and Laymeyer (1981 [383]) concluded that the birth of the first child represents a unique stress and is correlated with depression more strongly than a second or third birth.

Kendell et al. (1976 [323]) reviewed 2,257 births in 1970 using the Camberwell Register and determined an unexpectedly high proportion of illegitimate births correlated with psychiatric symptoms. They concluded that women with illegitimate births were twice as likely to experience a new episode of "psychiatric morbidity" in the 9th trimester (1976:297). However, by comparing rates throughout the four-year study, they found no significantly higher rate for these women compared to the entire study group. Also, they concluded that neither still births or twin births were "particularly stressful" (1976:300).

Finally, Nilsson and Almgren using a wide range of personality tests, found no relationship between level of intelligence and the frequency of symptoms in the postpartum period (1970:102 [441]).

The data presented in the studies described above suggest that there may be a more complex causal pattern or chain involved in the etiology of postpartum depression than biologically based theories alone can encompass (see Table 2). However, the psychological literature in general has been plagued by some methodological problems which merit attention. For example, sample size has tended to be small and to utilize women who are still hospitalized postpartum, i.e., a clinical population, which may skew the data in terms of unique time, context and physiological contexts. Frate et al. note that such methodology may confuse reactions caused by hospitalization with the finding of depression associated with the third or fourth postpartum day prior to release: "Due to the fact that most research has been hospital-based, little is actually known about postpartum reactions outside the institutions" (1979:357 [190]).

Psychological studies have tended to focus on personality dysfunction as measured through such constructs as "depression," "anxiety," "tendermindedness," etc. Few studies have actually observed behavior, or interpreted the results of psychological tests in the context of the wider social system of the family or community.

While most of the psychological research on postpartum mental states has been based on the use of personality tests, i.e., the Maudsley Personality Inventory, Lubin's Depression Adjective Checklist, the Raskin Three-Area Depression Scale, TAT, etc., no tests have been specifically designed to measure depression associated with the complex conditions associated with childbirth. For example, on some personality tests "constipation" is used as a variable in measuring depression. However, iron supplements, which are routinely prescribed to women postpartum, often produce a side effect of constipation.

III. ANTHROPOLOGICAL PERSPECTIVES

The perinatal period--conception through childbirth and the postpartum--is everywhere differently segmented and defined structurally in terms of its behavioral, social, and experiential content. Perinatal events are not merely physiological sequences but reflect what Jordan has termed "biosocial" phenomena in which both the behavior and feelings of the woman, a well as those around her, are differentially patterned, segmented, emphasized, and ritually marked (Jordan, 1980:1 [304]). This patterning of perinatal events represents each society's "policies" about the importance of the perinatal period for the mother and child, the family, and the wider social system and reflects theories about the nature and implications of these events.

It has been assumed by anthropologists that events in the life cycle are structured or ritually marked (i.e., rites de passage) because they are problematic or mark a transition in social roles. The social recognition of these transitions assists the individual in successfully passing through them and assuming a new role. Specifically referring to childbirth, Van Gennep notes: "It is apparent that the physiological return from childbirth is not the primary consideration, but that instead there is a social return from childbirth..." (1960:46 [619]). Absence of such social recognition at critical life events or changes has been thought to contribute to difficulties in the form of negative mental health and/or social consequences (e.g., juvenile delinquency, teenage pregnancy, depression following bereavement, etc.). In the U.S., we do not typically structure or ritually recognize the transition into motherhood. That the postpartum period has become informally recognized as a time of negative experiences and emotions is evidenced by the extraordinarily high number of women who report feeling "blue" or depressed.

Interestingly, a review of the ethnographic literature on childbirth shows remarkably little evidence for postpartum depression in non-Western settings. For example, researching the influence of native customs on obstetrics in Nigeria among the Ibibio, Kelly states: "Postpartum depressions are rare. This may be due to the postpartum customs of the Ibibio people" (1967:611 [320]).

A study in southeast Asia found "...no unusual anxieties or apprehension" in the postpartum period (Hart, 1965:28 [257]).

In a study of 80 women from four castes in Nepal, Upreti noted that: "postpartum 'blues' or depression seems to be less prevalent among Nepalese than among many Westerners. The psycho-social support system available to Nepalese women may account for this discrepancy in mothers' feelings and behaviors" (1970:117). Upreti's (1979 [618]) study points to the cross-cultural variation in which segments of the perinatal period are emphasized. In contrast to the U.S., where we accord great attention to the pregnancy and see childbirth as its culmination, in Nepal pregnancy goes almost unacknowledged while the postpartum period is carefully structured with sequential rituals and shared notions of appropriate behaviors and feelings.

Stephenson et al., after a review of the literature on Micronesia and informal interviews with 21 informants, hypothesize that postpartum depression is not common in Micronesia (Stephenson, Huxzel, and Harui-Walsh, 1979:3 [582]).

In research on the postpartum period ("doing the month") in China, Pillsbury found no evidence of postpartum depression, and suggests the importance of social support in the postpartum:

> My observations of interpersonal inter-
> action in Chinese households during the month
> give the impression that far more attention is
> lavished upon the mother, relative to the newborn
> infant, than in the U.S. This extra attention
> their families and social networks show them
> while doing the month seems, in fact, to preclude
> Chinese women from experiencing postpartum
> depression as understood and so taken for
> granted by Americans--despite the fact that
> the same biological factors are operative for
> women in both cultural backgrounds. (1978:18 481])

Before interpreting these findings positively, there are several methodological caveats. First, the absence of evidence for postpartum depression cross-culturally may reflect the lack of attention given to pregnancy by anthropologists until relatively recently (e.g., Jordan, 1980 [304]; Cosminsky, 1977 [131]; Mead and Newton, 1967 [400]; Pillsbury, 1978 [481]; MacCormack, 1982 [376]). It has been suggested that this lack of interest results from a predominance of male researchers who may have overlooked these issues because of: 1) lack of interest, or 2) lack of access to information in traditionally female domains (Jordan, 1980:5 [304]; Mead and Newton, 1967:151 [400]).

Second, there are no cross-cultural studies which present either diagnostic information acceptable to clinicians or the degree of social context information deemed necessary by anthropologists for the interpretation of behavior. Thus, we lack both formal testing as well as field observations of postpartum emotional states. Cross-cultural comparisons and assessment will be made even more difficult in this area because of the confounding of behavioral and experiential (emotional) criteria in the Western conceptualization of "depression." This mixture of the behavioral manifestations and internal feeling or emotional states in the notion of depression is problematic even within a Western context:

> The specific emotional responses during the postpartum period have usually been referred to as an actual depression syndrome. However, manifestation of specific behavioral responses does not necessarily equal a clinical diagnosis of depression, but rather only behavioral characteristics which can be associated with that psychological disorder. (Frate et al., 1979:356 [190]).

The complexity of these issues is seen in a study by Davidson (1972 [156]) of 43 Jamaican women. Using standardized diagnostic instruments (Beck Depression Scale and Taylor Manifest Anxiety Scale), these women were found to have the highest levels of depression not after but during pregnancy, although 26 women (60.4%) also experienced emotional upset in the first 11 days postpartum, mostly in days 1-3 (1972:660). The importance of the wider social context in interpreting these findings, however, is seen by further description of the women as poor, high parity, living in a general situation of high unemployment, with lack of institutionalized marriage or mandated financial or emotional support from the baby's father (1972:662).

Finally, the ethnographic descriptions available tend to be trait cluster analyses (c.f. Mead and Newton, 1967 [400]; Ford, 1945 [187]; Naroll, Naroll & Howard, 1961 [433]) or to be vague about method, sample size, elicitation techniques, and informant characteristics, making it difficult to evaluate statements about the existence of postpartum depression.

Cautioned by these methodological problems and gaps in the literature, the possibility remains that behaviors that are categorized as postpartum depression in the West--forms of moderate depression or "baby blues"--are not widely found cross-culturally and represent in effect a culture-bound syndrome (for an in-depth review of this hypothesis see Stern & Kruckman, 1983 [584]).

IV. SUMMARY

Most research and treatment of postpartum depression has focused on the more serious psychotic reactions. The consistently recorded low rates for this form historically and cross-culturally suggest that it may represent a discrete clinical entity or illness. In contrast, very high incidence rates for milder forms of postpartum depression-- in the U.S. popularly known as "baby blues"--have received little attention from researchers due to the perception that this phenomenon is "ubiquitous" (Yalom et al., 1968:16 [655]), "inevitable" (Frate et al., 1979:355 [190]), and self-limiting.

A review of the psychiatric literature on postpartum depression shows the overwhelming emphasis on biological explanations based on the global hormonal changes occurring postpartum. The precise mechanisms which would produce the clinical syndrome of psychotic depression or its milder forms have not been identified. It may be that "baby blues" may simply be the milder end of a biologically based continuum in which the severe end is psychosis. It may be that lumping the various forms of depression together at all is a conceptual mistake; e.g., perhaps psychotic postpartum depression is simply a form of manic-depressive illness with a postpartum onset. As with affective disorders in general, the relative importance of biological, social and psychological factors in etiology remains debated.

Research on the psychological correlates of postpartum depression has serious methodological limitations: most studies are based on an in-hospital sample and results are thus confounded by the effects of hospitalization. In addition, the lack of prospective or long-term follow-up studies makes reported mental status in the immediate postpartum a questionable measure. Finally, psychological studies have suggested correlates, such as maternal age, environmental stress, etc., but the specific ways in which these variables relate to depression are unclear.

The phenomenon of mild postpartum depression remains undocumented in the cross-cultural literature, yet this lack of documentation, in contrast to high incidence rates in the U.S. and other industrialized nations, suggests the possibility that it is an example of a "culture-bound" syndrome.

This review and bibliography will, we hope, stimulate research in several new directions. But, most important, our aim is to encourage a union between biogenic and psychogenic research, including research in the context of the family and community. To pursue isolated research in biology or psychology seems limited. What is needed are more longitudinal studies utilizing biological and social variables. We also hope this review will provide easy access to materials from diverse disciplines.

V.   BIBLIOGRAPHY FRAMEWORK

Several information systems were used in the search of the literature including the National Library of Medicine, MEDLINE, National Clearinghouse for Mental Health Information, and the Human Relations Area File. Because diverse disciplines (i.e., biochemistry, nursing, medicine, anthropology) have been concerned with postpartum depression research and treatment, additional manual searches were made to expand the listings. Additional sources, especially many of the international listings, were provided through correspondence. The bibliography is an alphabetical listing of recent and important historical articles from all disciplines. MEDLINE abbreviations have been used when possible. There are selected annotations of the most recent and widely quoted articles from various disciplines. The annotations are divided into sections that reflect the following:

1. type of study employed;
2. method of obtaining data and size of a study population;
3. methodology;
4. definition of postpartum depression utilized;
5. criteria used for diagnosing depression;
6. results of the study;
7. treatment plan employed or offered.

One or more of the categories may be omitted due to the nature of the study. For example, if number 4 is not in the annotation it means the information was not provided in the article or does not apply.

Following the bibliography are two comprehensive indexes: first there is a subject index providing the user with articles with information such as scales used to measure depression, predictive scales, incidence, etc. This is followed by a geographical/cultural index allowing the user to examine various theories of etiology in non-Western settings.

TABLE 1. The Symptomatology, Time of Onset, and Incidence of Three Levels of Post-Partum Depression

LEVEL OF DEPRESSION	SYMPTOMS	ONSET	TIME/SOURCE OF STUDY	INCIDENCE RATE
Postpartum psychosis (puerperal psychosis): organic, schizophrenic; depressive (most common); and mania	Delirium, hallucinations, fatigue coupled with diminished thinking and response, rapid mood change, agitation, confusion	Acute and quick onset, (80% of all cases occur between 3-14 days)	-Connolly's 1846 study (see Crickshank, 1940:571) [142]	1 per 1000 births
			-Jone's (1902:579) review of London's Lunacy Commission data [301]	1 per 1100
			-Hemphill's (1952:158) analysis of 1930 research [265]	.25 per 1000
			-Ostwald's (1957:153) U.S. study during the 1950's [463]	2 per 1000
			-Butt's (1969:136) summary of research in the 1960's [107]	1 per 1000
			-Recent research by Brown and Shereshefsky (1972:157) [95] and Balchin (1975:41) [33]	1 per 1000
Moderate depression disorder (depressive neurosis)	Feelings of inadequacy, guilt, anxiety, fatigue, tearfulness, and irritability	Variable onset, any- time from 2 weeks to 3 months	-Frate et al. (1979) [190]	30-200 per 1000
			-Pitt (1975) [488]	
			-Tod (1971) [608]	
			-Dalton (1971)[145]	
			-Nilsson and Almgren (1970) [441]	
			-Jacobson et al. (1965) [287]	
Transitory minor affec- tive disturbance (transitory "blues" or maternity "blues")	Irritability, mood changes, poor sleep, tearfulness	0-3rd day	-Handley's (1977) British study [246]	640 per 1000
			-Heitler's (1976) U.S. Research [264]	520 per 1000
			-Davidson's (1972) Study of Jamaican Women [156]	604 per 1000
			-Dalton's (1971) Study of Mothers with an imbalance in Proges- terone [145]	640 per 1000
			-Yalom's et al. (1968) Study of multiparous Women [655]	730 per 1000
			-Kaij's et al. (1967) Swedish study [307]	600 per 1000
			-Hamilton's (1962) Review of U.S. research [245]	800 per 1000

xxxi

TABLE 2.   Theories of Etiology: Causes and Correlates

A.   HORMONAL LINK

   - Progesterone level drops from 140 ng/ml to 2 ng/ml 10 days after birth

      Hamilton, 1977 [245]
      Hytten and Leitch, 1964 [280]
      Nott et al., 1976 [450]

   - Estrogen level drops from 2100 ng/ml to 10 ng/ml on the 9th day after birth

      Hamilton, 1977 [245]
      Hytten and Leitch, 1964 [280]
      Nott et al., 1976 [450]

   - Elevated corticosteroids during pregnancy

      Hytten and Leitch, 1964 [280]

   - Elevated levels of prolactin on the 3rd post-partum day associated with the galactopoiesis and lactogenesis processes where the "blues" subside after the milk-let-down reflex

      Dalton, 1971 [145]
      Hytten and Leitch [280]
      Pitt, 1973 [487]

   - Elevated cyclic-AMP during the puerperium

      Ballinger et al., 1979 [36]

   - Pituitary thyroid hormone deficit

      Butts, 1969 [107]
      Hamilton, 1977 [245]

   - Lack of hormonal synchrony

      Treadway et al., 1969 [610]

   - Similar hormonal patterns in individuals with pre-menstral anxiety

      Malleson, 1963 [384]

B.   BIOLOGICAL LINK

   - Menstrual cycle distress.

      Dalton, 1971 [145]
      Malleson, 1963 [384]
      Yalom et al., 1968 [655]

   - Shortened gestation

      Jackson and Laymeyer, 1981 [283]

xxxii

TABLE 2. (Cont.)

- Increased number of physical symptoms during pregnancy

    Paffenbarger, 1964 [464]

- Labor complications and fetal distress

    Robson and Kumer, 1980 [517]
    Paffenbarger, 1964 [464]

- Parity (higher/lower)

    Davidson, 1972 [156]
    Jackson and Laymeyer, 1981 [283]

- Sleep disorder

    Karacan, 1969 [315]

- Conception in March, February, October or January

    Grundy et al., 1975 [229]

- Consanguineal relative with a psychiatric disturbance

    Reich and Winokur, 1970 [503]

C. PSYCHOLOGICAL LINK

- Poor relationship with mother

    Heitler, 1976 [264]
    Douglas, 1963 [171]

- Lack of companionship

    Pitt, 1968 [487]
    Stahlie, 1960 [579]

- Inadequate housing

    Pitt, 1968 [487]
    Nilsson and Almgren, 1970 [441]

- High level of geographical mobility

    Heitler, 1976 [264]

- Reduced social support network

    Nilsson and Almgren, 1970 [441]
    Pitt, 1968 [487]
    Robson and Kumer, 1980 [517]
    Yalom, 1968 [655]

TABLE 2. (Concl.)

- Age of mother

    Frate et al., 1979 [190]
    Kendell et al., 1976 [323]
    Sosa et al., 1980 [576]
    Uddenberg, 1975 [655]

- Poor marital relationship

    Heitler, 1976 [264]
    Nilsson and Almgren, 1970 [441]
    Pitt, 1968 [487]
    Sosa Et al., 1980 [576]

- Ambivalence concerning pregnancy

    Nilsson and Almgren, 1970 [441]
    Sosa et al., 1980 [576]

- Sexual identity conflict

    Brown and Shereshefsky, 1972 [95]

- Illegitimate child

    Kendall et al., 1976 [323]

- Postpartum emotional problems in father, adoptive parents, or grandmother

    Asch and Rubin, 1974 [18]
    Ginath, 1974 [209]

Postpartum Depression

1. Abely, P., and R. Bouguet.
   1962 "Nouvel essai de delimitation des
   psychoses dites puerperals." ANN. MED.
   PSYCH. 120 Annee, T. II:364-385.

2. Adams, F.
   1886 THE GENUINE WORKS OF HIPPOCRATES.
   New York: William Wood & Co. Volume 1.

3. Affonso, Dyanne.
   1977 "Missing Pieces--A Study of
   Postpartum Feelings." BIRTH AND THE
   FAMILY J. 4(4):159-164.

4. Aitken, J.M.
   1911 "The Insanities of the Puerperal
   Period." WEST. M. REV. 14:10-14.

5. Albretsen, C.S.
   1968 "Hospitalization of Postpartum
   Psychotic Patients Together with Babies
   and Husbands." ACTA PSYCHIAT. SCAND.
   203:179-182.

6. Alder, E.M., and J.L. Cox.
   1983 "Breastfeeding and Postnatal
   Depression." J. PSYCHOSOM.
   27(2):139-144.

7. Alfonson, D.D.
   1982 "Assessment of Women's Postpartal
   Adaptation as Indicator of Vulnerability
   to Depression." DISS. ABSTR. University
   of Arizona.

   1) Prospective. 2) 80 mothers selected
   from regional birthing centers. 3) Using
   a variety of tests mothers were
   interviewed three and eight weeks
   postpartum. 5) Beck's Depression Scale,
   Pitt's Questionnaire, Maternal Assessment

Scale, and Psychological Screening
Inventory. 6) Several aspects of
postpartum adaptation are significantly
related with depression. Variables with
highest correlation include: mood, sleep
and eating schedule, energy levels, and
negative emotions towards infants.

8. AMERICAN JOURNAL OF OBSTETRICS AND
   GYNECOLOGY, EDITORS OF.
   1957 "The Clinical Issues of Postpartum
   Psychopathological Reactions."
   73:305-312.

9. Ammar, S.
   1962 "Psycho-organic Disorders of
   Pregnancy, Childbirth, and Breastfeeding
   in Tunisia (and Generally in Countries
   with a High Birth Rate)." LA TUNISIE
   MEDICALE 1-2, January-February.

10. Anderson, E.W.
    1933 "A Study of the Sexual Life in
    Psychoses Associated with Childbirth."
    J. MENT. SCI. 79:137-149.

11. Anderson, Edith.
    1963 "A Study of the Relationship Between
    Depression and Interpersonal Conflict in
    the Postpartum." Unpublished
    Dissertation. New York University, New
    York.

12. Anthony, E.J.
    1959 "A Group of Murderous Mothers." ACTA
    PSYCHOTHERAPY SUPPL. 7(2):1-6.

13. Arboleda-Florez, Julio.
    1975 "Infanticide: Some Medicolegal
    Considerations." CANADIAN PSYCHIAT.
    ASSOC. J. 20(1):55-60.

14. Arentsen, K.
    1968 "Postpartum Psychoses." DANISH MED
    BULL. 15(4):97-100.

15. Areskog, Barb, Nils Uddenberg, and Beendt
    Kjessler.
    1984 "Postnatal Emotional Balance in Women
    with and without Fear of Childbirth."
    J. PYSCHOSOM. RESEARCH 28(3):213-220.

16. Armstrong-Jones, R.
    1923 "Puerperal Insanity." LANCET
    1:1296-1298.

17. Asch, S.W.
    1968 "Crib Deaths: Their Possible Relation
    to Postpartum Depression and
    Infanticide." MT. SINAI J. MED.
    35:214-220.

18. Asch, Stuart S., and Lowell J. Rubin.
    1974 "Postpartum Reactions: Some
    Unrecognized Variations." AM. J.
    PSYCHIAT. 131(8):870-874.

    1) Summary. 6) Asch's review of four
    cases supports the idea that postpartum
    reactions are primarily psychogenic
    because depression occurs in subjects who
    did not give birth: grandmother, father,
    adoption mothers.

19. Aschaffenburg, G.
    1901 "Ueber die klinischen FORMEN der
    Wochenbettpsychosen." ALLG. ZTSCHR.
    PSYCHIAT. 58:337-356.

20. Assael, M.I.; J.M. Nambose; G.A. German;
    and F.J. Bennett.
    1972 "Psychiatric Disturbances During
    Pregnancy in a Rural Group of African
    Women." SOC. SCI. MED. 6(3):387-395.

21. Astrachan, J.M.
    1965 "Severe Psychological Disorders in
    the Puerperium." OBSTET. GYNEC.
    25:13-25.

22. Atkinson, Ann K.
    1980 "Postpartum Depression in Primiparous
    Parents: Caretaking Demands and
    Prepartum Expectations." DISS. ABSTR.
    INTL. 40(11-B):5396.

23. _____.
    1984 "Postpartum Depression in Primiparous
    Parents." J. ABNORMAL PSYCHOL.
    93(1):115-119.

    1) Prospective. 2) 78 Primiparous couples
    recruited through private physicians and
    childbirth classes. 3) Questionnaires
    assessing stress were completed at 8 weeks
    prepartum and 8 weeks postpartum. These
    include: a Personal and Social History
    Questionnaire; Inventory of Caregiving
    Behavior; Neonatal Perception Inventory;
    Degree of Bother Inventory; Pleasant
    Events Schedule- -Mood Related Scale; and
    the Beck Depression Inventory. 5) Beck
    Depression Inventory. 6) Results
    indicated that when the level of prepartum
    depression was controlled, positively
    reinforcing events were negatively related
    to postpartum depression in women. For
    men, the degree to which their infant's
    behavior was viewed as "Better than
    average" was negatively related to
    postpartum depression. Findings were
    consistant with the behavioral
    theories interpretation of postpartum.

24. _____.
    1984 "Postpartum Depression in Primiparous
        Parents -- Note." ABNORMAL PSYCHIATRY
        93(1):115-119.

25. Aukamp, Virginia.
    1984 NURSING CARE PLANS FOR THE
        CHILDBEARING FAMILY. Norwalk, Conn.:
        Appleton-Century-Crofts.

    1) Care plans with recommendations for
    nursing interventions. 7) This series of
    care plans like many others develops care
    plans for the postpartum period. However,
    suggested follow-up includes areas such as
    nutritional needs and other biological
    concerns such as lactation and body
    weight. Only two care plans concern
    social or psychological topics: body image
    and sibling rivalry. While these plans
    include valuable interventions and
    criteria for measuring outcome much more
    is needed regarding the prevention and
    treatment of the mother and spouses'
    emotional concerns.

26. Avant, Patricia C.
    1979 "Maternal Attachment and Anxiety: An
        Exploratory Study." DISS. ABSTR. INTL.
        40(1-B):165.

27. Ayres, Barbara C.
    1967 "Pregnancy Magic: A Study of Food
        Taboos and Sex Avoidances." In:
        CROSS-CULTURAL APPROACHES: READINGS IN
        COMPARATIVE RESEARCH. (Clelland S.
        Ford, ed.) New Haven: Human Relations
        Area Files Press. pp. 111-125.

28. Bagedahl-Strindlund, M., and B. Jansson.
    1983 "Does the Season of Conception
        Influence the Frequency of Post Partum
        Mental Illness?" ACTA PSYCHIAT. SCAND.
        67:159-162.

    1) Summary. 2) Two Studies, 71 women in
    1952--56; and 68 women in 1976--77. 3)
    The month of conception was estimated by
    adding 14 days to the date of the first
    day of the last menstrual cycle. 6) No
    statistically significant patterns were
    found.

29. Baker, A.A.
    1967 Psychiatric Disorders in Obstetrics.
        Oxford and Edinburgh: Blackwell
        Scientific Publication.

    1) Summary. 2) Personal observation and
    research of women attending a mother and
    baby unit in Banstead. 6) The spectrum of
    puerperal mental illnesses--neurosis and
    organic and functional psychoses--is
    discussed. Stress is placed on the
    importance of family members in eliciting
    relevant data concerning symptoms, in
    understanding the etiology of the
    illnesses, and the subsequent treatment
    strategy. Author offers various forms of
    treatment: Psycho-social, psychotropic
    and psychotherapeutic.

30. _____.
    1969 "Psychiatric Illness in Parents."
        NURS. MIRROR AND MIDWIVES J.
        128(16):37-39.

31. Baker, A.A., et al.
    1961 "Admitting Schizophrenic Mothers with
        Their Babies." LANCET 543:237-239.

32. Baker, Max; Joe Dorzab; and George
    Winokur.
    1971 "Depressive Disease: The Effect of
    the Postpartum State." BIOL. PSYCHIAT.
    3(4):357-365.

    1) Retrospective--prospective. 2) 100
    depressive mothers and 129 relatives. 3)
    Structured interviews as well as detailed
    history concerning number of pregnancy,
    outcome, and the occurrence of associated
    psychiatric symptoms. 4) A postpartum
    depressive episode was defined as a
    persistent depressive syndrome lasting a
    minimum of six weeks whose onset was
    within six months of the time giving
    birth. 5) Reich and Winokur Scale. 6)
    First study to systematically investigate
    postpartum depression in affective
    disorder patients who manifest only
    depression. 6% of the sample (N=65)
    experienced depression. The rate of
    morbidity risk was not significantly
    different than the risk at any other time
    during the childbearing years. Unipolar
    patients had much less frequent affective
    disorders than bipolar patients.

33. Balchin, P.
    1975 "The Midwife and Puerperal
    Psychosis." MIDWIFE HEALTH VISITOR
    7(2):41-43.

    1) Commentary. 4) Any condition which
    gives rise to a conflict about childbirth,
    resulting in an increase of mental strain,
    which may result in a psychotic reaction.
    7) The midwife's role is one of
    prevention. Once the puerperal psychosis
    has developed, it is similar to other
    mental breakdowns. Therefore the

prognosis and treatment of puerperal
depressive states necessitates the
patient's admission to a hospital. The
midwife, through empathy, can provide
effective care above and beyond
traditional treatment modes.

34. Balduzzi, Edoardo.
    1951 "La psychose puerperale: Essai
    d'interpretation pathogenique."
    L'ENCEPHALE 401:11-43.

35. Ballarchey, E.L.; D.G. Campbell; B.
    Claffey; R. Escamilla; A.W. Footer; J.A.
    Hamilton; J.M. Harter; A.B. Litteral;
    H.M. Lyons; E.W. Overstreet; P.P.
    Poliak; K.L. Schaupp Jr.; G. Smith; and
    A.T. Voris.
    1958 "Response of Postpartum Psychiatric
    Symptoms to 1-Triiodothyronine." J.
    CLIN. EXPER. PSYCHOPATH. 19:170.

36. Ballinger, B.C.; D.E. Buckley; G.J.
    Naylor; and D.A. Stansfield.
    1979 "Emotional Disturbance Following
    Childbirth: Clinical Findings and
    Urinary Excretion of Cyclic AMP."
    PSYCHOL. MED. 9(2):293-300.

1) Prospective (with a summary). 2) 109
women who volunteered on day of delivery.
The mean age was 25; 41% were primiparas.
3) The subjects were interviewed within 24
hours after birth and 48 hours later using
a semi-structured interview schedule.
Later, the subjects were interviewed at
two months and at 1 year after delivery
using the General Health Questionnaire,
GHQ (self-administered). 5) Two groups
were assembled according to their GHQ
score: elated and depressed. It was with

these groups that urinary excretion of
cyclic AMP was compared. 6) Emotional
"disturbance" was found to be at its
highest immediately after delivery and
then gradually decreased. Levels of cyclic
AMP in urine was not found to be a
significant indicator of etiology.

37. Ballinger, Barbara C.
    1982 "Emotional Disturbance During
    Pregnancy and Following Delivery."   J.
    PSYCHOSOM. RES. 26(6):629-634.

38. Bardon, D.
    1968 "Mother and Baby Unit: Psychiatric
    Survey of 115 Cases." BR. MED. J.
    2:755-758.

39. _____.
    1973 "Psychological Implications of
    Provision for Childbirth." LANCET
    555:2.

40. _____.
    1977 "A Mother and Baby Unit in a
    Psychiatric Hospital." NURS. MIRROR
    145:23-30.

41. Barker, F.
    1883 THE PUERPERAL DISEASES. 4th Edition.
    New York: Appleton.

42. Barnes, D.J.
    1975 "The Aftermath of Childbirth Physical
    Aspects." PROC. R. SOC. MED. 68(4):223.

43. Bartels, Lampart.
    1969 "Birth Customs and Birth Songs of the
    Macha Galla." ETHNOLOGY 8:406-422.

44. Barzilai, S.H., and A.M. Davies.
    1972 "Postpartum Mental Disorders in
    Jerusalem: Survey of Hospitalized Cases
    1964-1967." BR. J. SOC. PSYCHIAT. COMM.
    HEALTH 6(2):80-89.

45. Beaudoin, Marc A.
    1981 "Prediction of Postpartum Maternal
    Self-Esteem by Demographic Data,
    Personality, Attitude, Pregnancy and
    Childbirth Variables." DISS. ABSTR.
    INTL. 42(1-B):363.

46. Beckmann, E.
    1939 "Ueber Zustandsbilder und Verlaufe
    von Puerperalpsychosen." ALLG. ZTSCHR.
    PSYCHIAT. 113:239-293.

47. Beeman, W.O., and A.K. Bhattacharyya.
    1978 "Toward an Assessment of the Social
    Role of Rural Midwives and Its
    Implications for the Family Planning
    Program: An Iranian Case Study." HUMAN
    ORG. 37(3):295-301.

48. Bell, Richard Q.
    1975 "Reduction of the Stress in
    Child-Rearing." In: SOCIETY, STRESS
    AND DISEASE. Volume II: CHILDHOOD AND
    ADOLESCENCE. (Lennart Levi, ed).
    London: Oxford Univ. Press. pp. 416-421.

49. Bensel, R.W., and C.L. Paxson, Jr.
    1977 "Child Abuse Following Postpartum
    Separation." J. PEDIATRICS
    90(3):490-491.

1) Retrospective. 2) 438 neonates from
Hennepen County 1970 special care nursery.
3) Infants were screened for levels of
abuse. Abused babies were compared to a

control group. 6) Results do not support
previously recorded conclusions that child
abuse is associated with preterm delivery,
lenghty nursery hospitalization,
infrequent maternal nursery visits,
separation of mother and infant during
first six months, or illness in the
child's first year. However, maternal
gestational illness and postpartum
separation are associated with child
abuse.

50. Bibring, G.
    1959 "Some Considerations of the
    Psychological Processes in Pregnancy."
    PSYCHOANAL. STUDY CHILD 14:113-121.

51. _____ .
    1961 "A Study of the Psychological
    Processes in Pregnancy and of the
    Earliest Mother-Child Relationship."
    PSYCHOANAL. STUDY CHILD 16:9-45.

52. Bibring, G.; T. Dwyer; D. Huntington; and
    A. Valenstein.
    1961 "A Study of the Earliest Mother-Child
    Relationship." PSYCHOANAL. STUDY CHILD
    16:9-72.

53. Bibring, G., and A. Valenstein.
    1976 "Psychological Aspects of Pregnancy."
    CLIN. OBSTET. GYNECOL. 19(2):357-371.

54. Bieber, Irving, and Toby B. Bieber.
    1978 "Post-Partum Reactions in Men and
    Women." J. AM. ACAD. PSYCHOANAL.
    6(4):511-519.

55. Billig, O., and J.D. Bradley.
1946 "Combined Shock and Corpus Luteum
Hormone Therapy." AM. J. PSYCHIAT.
102:783-787.

56. Billman, A., and F. Zalk.
1978 EXPECTANT FATHERS. New York:
Hawthorne Books.

57. Bisi, Ricardo H.
1956 "Dermatosis in a Case of Postpartum
Psychosis." PSYCHOANAL. QUART.
25:348-356.

58. Blair, R.A., et al.
1970 "Puerperal Depression. A Study of
Predictive Factors." ROY. COLL. GEN.
PRACT. 19:22-25.

59. Blaker, Karen, and L. Pfanku.
1974 "Self-Disclosure and Depression
During the Antepartum and Postpartum
Periods Among Primiparous Spouses."
DISS. ABSTR. INT. 34(12-B):6190.

60. Bledin, K.D., and B. Brice.
1983 "Psychological Conditions in
Pregnancy and the Puerperium and Their
Relevance to Postpartum Sterilization -
A Review." BULLETIN WORLD HEALTH
ORGANIZATION 61(3):533-544.

61. Bleek, W.
1976 "Spacing of Children, Sexual
Abstinence, and Breast Feeding in Rural
Ghana." SOC. SCI. MED. 10(5):225-230.

62. Blum, Harold P.
1978 "Reconstruction in a Case of
Postpartum Depression." PSYCHOANAL.
STUDY CHILD 33:335-362.

63. Blumberg, A., and O. Billig.
    1942 "Hormonal Influence Upon 'Puerperal
    Psychosis' and Neurotic Conditions: A
    Modification of Insulin Shock
    Treatment." PSYCHIAT. QUART.
    16:454-462.

64. Blumberg, Nancy Long.
    1979 "Early Maternal Postpartum
    Adjustment: A Study of the Effects of
    Neonatal Risk, Maternal Attitude Toward
    Pregnancy and Childbirth, and Maternal
    Cognitive Style." DISS. ABSTR. INTL.
    39(12-B):6108.

65. _____.
    1980 "Effects of Neonatal Risk, Maternal
    Attitude, and Cognitive Style on Early
    Postpartum Adjustment." J. ABNORMAL
    PSYCHOL. 89(2):139-150.

66. Bobak, I.M., and M. Jensen.
    1984 ESSENTIALS OF MATERNAL NURSING. St.
    Louis: C.V. Mosby.

1) Summary/planning and care plan
implementation. 6) Chapter 39 focuses on
psychosocial risk factors and provides a
clear discription of symptoms and
treatment, including manic-depressive
psychosis and schizophrenia. Chapter 32
states that physical screening of new
mothers has been well developed but that
tools predicting high-risk parenting
behaviors are still imprecise. The authors
provide assessment tools for the first 5
days postpartum and for 2, 4, and 6 weeks
postpartum. The tools are concise allowing
easy application that can be used for
nursing diagnoses. Chapter 33 discusses
planning and implementation of nursing

14

actions. For each stage their guidelines provide information regarding initiating the relationship, consolidating the relationship and promoting growth in the parental role; helpful tools in providing care during the postpartum period.

67. Bogren, L.Y.
    1983 "Couvade." ACTA PSYCHIATR. SCAND.
    68:55-65.

68. _____.
    1984 "The Couvade Syndrome: Background
    Variables." ACTA PSYCHIATR. SCAND.
    70(4):316-320.

69. Bondeau, F.
    1977 "Puerperal Depression in
    Family-Practice." UNION MEDICALE DU
    CANADA 106:1137-1140.

70. BOSTON WOMEN'S HEALTH BOOK COLLECTIVE.
    1976 OUR BODIES, OUR SELVES. 2nd Edition.
    New York: Simon and Schuster.

71. Boszormenyi, Z., and A. Villeneuve.
    1974 "A Comparative Study of Psychoses
    Following Childbirth in Hungary and
    Quebec." CONFINIA PSYCHIATRICA
    17(2):111-121.

1) Retrospective. 2) One hundred case histories of patients treated at Central State Hospital for Nervous and Mental Disorders, Budapest, and an equal number of cases treated at Hospital St.-Michael-Archange, Quebec, between 1953 and 1969 were randomly selected for this study. 4) The postpartum was defined as birth to six months. 5) Diagnostic

criteria were developed after Conrad
(1960). Diagnosis using these
classifications were made by reviewing
recorded symptoms. Further control was
possible because authors had been the
attending physicians in the majority of
the cases at their respective hospitals.
6) The frequency of the different
classifications was similar except the
combined emotional-hyperesthetic and
phobic-anancastic classifications were
higher in Hungarians (p < 0.05). Mean age
of first onset was not significantly
different. However, a psychotic reaction
occured significantly more frequently in
primiparae and in grand multiparae French
Canadians. French Canadian women were more
seriously affected at time of
hospitalization than Hungarian women. "In
both countries, the diagnoses of puerperal
or postpartum psychosis seems to have
often been made as a protective gesture
against the cultural prejudice toward
major psychoses, such as schizophrenia and
manic-depressive psychosis." 7) Common
treatment approaches included ECT and
psychotropic drugs. The outcome was
similar in both studies but the
effectiveness was not stated.

72. Bourne, A.W.
    1924 "Aetiology and Prognosis of Puerperal
       Insanity." J. OBST. GYNAEC. BR. EMP.
       31:251-257.

73. Bower, Willis H., and Mark D. Altschule.
    1956 "Use of Progesterone in the Treatment
       of Postpartum Psychosis." NEW ENGL. J.
       MED. 254(4):157-160.

74. Boyd, D.A. Jr.
    1942 "Mental Disorders Associated with
         Childbearing." AM. J. OBSTET. GYNEC.
         43:148-165, 335-348.

75. Brandon, Sydney.
    1972 "Psychiatric Illness in Women." NURS.
         MIRROR AND MIDWIVES J. 134(3):17-18.

76. _____.
    1982 "Depression After Childbirth." BR.
         MED. J. 284:613-614.

77. Brandt, P.A.
    1984 "Stress Buffering Effects of Social
         Support on Maternal Discipline." NURS.
         RES. 33(4):229-234.

78. Bratfos, O., and J. O. Haug.
    1966 "Puerperal Mental Disorders in
         Manic-Depressive Females." ACTA
         PSYCHIAT. SCAND. 42:285-294.

79. Braverman, J., and J.F. Roux.
    1978 "Screening For Patient at Risk for
         Postpartum Depression." OBSTET. GYNEC.
         52(6):731-736.

80. Brazelton, T.B.
    1963 "The Early Mother-Infant Adjustment."
         PEDIATRICS. 32:931.

81. _____.
    1972 "Implications of Infant Development
         Among the Mayan Indians of Mexico."
         HUMAN DEVEL. 15:90-111.

82. _____.
    1973 "Effect of Maternal Expectations on
         Early Infant Behavior." EARLY CHILD
         DEV. CARE 2:259-273.

83. Brazelton, T.B.; B. Koslowski; and M.
    Main.
    1974 " The Origins of Reciprocity: The
    Early Mother-Infant Interaction." In:
    THE EFFECT OF THE INFANT ON ITS
    CAREGIVER. (M. Lewis and L.A.
    Rosenblum, eds.) New York: John Wiley &
    Sons.

84. Breen, D.
    1978 "The Mother and the Hospital." In:
    TEARING THE VEIL. (S. Lipshitz, ed.),
    pp. 17-35.

85. Brenner, A.K.
    1979 "The Blues." AM. BABY 41(5):50-56.

86. Brew, Mary F., and Robert Seidenberg.
    1950 "Psychotic Reactions Associated with
    Pregnancy and Childbirth." J. NERV. &
    MENT. DIS. 111:408-423.

87. Brewer, C.
    1977 "Incidence of Post-Abortion
    Psychosis: A Prospective Study." BR.
    MED. J. 1:476-477.

88. BRITISH MEDICAL JOURNAL.
    1979 "Postnatal Depression: Does Anyone
    Care?" II:1487-1488.

89. Brockington, I.F., et al.
    1978 A clinical study of post-partum
    psychosis. In: MENTAL ILLNESS IN
    PREGNANCY AND THE PUERPERIUM (Edited by
    M. Sandler). Oxford, London: Oxford
    University Press.

90. _____.
1981 "Puerperal Psychosis: Phenomena and Diagnosis." ARCHS. GEN. PSYCHIAT. 24:441-46. (England)

1) Prospective. 2) 56 women who were admitted to a hospital and were found to have had the onset of their illness within 2 weeks postpartum. 3) A control group comprised of 52 female psychotic patients from the same hospital between the ages of 17 and 37. 5) 5 separate methods were used to compare the experimental and control groups: a) interviewed with a Structural Mental State Inventory, b) an interview with the nearest relative, c) a standardized videotape interview, d) a self-rating on their present state of mind, e) nurse observations made using a rating procedure. All except self-questionnaires were given during first month after admission. 6) Only 5 of 58 episodes met schizophrenia criteria. The results are interpreted as supporting a link between puerperal psychosis and manic-depressive disease.

91. Brown, George W., and Susan Davidson.
1978 "Social Class, Psychiatric Disorder of Mother and Accidents to Children." LANCET 1(8060):378-380.

92. Brown, George W., and T. Harris.
1978 THE SOCIAL ORIGINS OF DEPRESSION: A STUDY OF PSYCHIATRIC DISORDERS IN WOMEN. London: Tavistock Publication.

93. Brown, Harris P.
1973 "Social Supports Can Protect Against Depression." PSYCHOL. MED. 12:159-60.

94. Brown, Walter A.
    1979 PSYCHOLOGICAL CARE DURING PREGNANCY
        AND THE POSTPARTUM PERIOD. New York:
        Raven Press.

95. Brown, Walter A., and Pauline
        Shereshefsky.
    1972 "Seven Women: A Prospective Study of
        Postpartum Psychiatric Disorders."
        PSYCHIATRY 35(2):139-158.

96. Browne, William J., and Anthony J. Palmer.
    1975 "A Preliminary Study of Schizophrenic
        Women Who Murdered Their Children."
        HOSP. COMM. PSYCHIAT. 26(2):71,5.

97. Browner, C.
    1980 "Machismo, Sympathetic Pregnancy, and
        Changing Men's Roles in Urban Colombia."
        Paper Presented at Annual Meetings of
        the American Anthropological
        Association, November.

98. Brush, E.N.
    1899 "Does Sepsis Play a Prominent
        Causative Role in the Production of
        Puerperal Insanity?" AM. MED. QUART.
        (New York) 1:141-144.

99. Buchwald, J., and R. Unterman.
    1981 "Predicting Postpartum Depression."
        CLIN. RES. 29(5):842.

1) Retrospective. 2) 31 Women with a
clinically proven diagnosis of postpartum
depression were interviewed. 3) Authors
sought to identify personality
characteristics in women that place them
at high risk for the development of
postpartum depression. 6) The
investigation uncovered 27 prepartum

personality and experiential characteristics that were present in most of the women. These characteristics were essentially psychological in nature and indicated that almost all women with postpartum depression gave a history of a disturbed relationship with both parents as well as previous evidence of maladaption. 7) A questionnaire based on these findings could be administered during the antepartum period to identify women at high risk for postpartum depression.

100. _____.
1982 "Precursors and Predictors of Postpartum Depression: A Retrospective Study." J. PREVENTIVE PSYCHIATRY 1(3):293-308.

1) Retrospective. 2) 31 Women with clinically proven diagnoses of moderate-to-severe depression that originated during the first 6 weeks postpartum were interviewed. 3) Most women were selected randomly from the postpartum and well baby clinics. Some were also selected through referrals from obstetricians, social workers, and mental health therapists. 5) DSM-III criteria. 6) Early patient-mother relationship was found to be the best source of prediction. Lack of support from husband and siblings also played a role in the development of postpartum depression along with previous emotional and behavioral disorders. The authors also found an excessive moralizing attitude toward sex in the parental homes of postpartum depressed women. 80% of the women had seriously disturbing

relationships with their fathers. 7) They suggest the possibility of developing a questionnaire to be given to antepartum women to identify high-risk patients. This would allow health care personnel to recommend psychotherapeutic and social intervention to ease or prevent the devastating effects of postpartum depression on patient and family.

101. Bucove, S.
1964 "Postpartum Psychoses in the American Male." BULL. NY. MED. 40:961-971.

102. Bull, Margaret, and Donna Lawrence.
1985 "Mothers' Use of Knowledge During the First Postpartum Weeks." JOGN. 14(4):315-20.

1) Point study. 2) 78 mothers were provided a self-administered questionnaire during their hospital stay. 3) Questionnaire was developed to measure what information re: self care and infant care mothers found useful. 6) In view of shorter hospital stays authors found it important to know what information and resources for new mothers would be useful. Needs seemed to focus on physical self-care, i.e.,clothing, diet, cleansing, decrease in vaginal flow, lifting and sexual activity. Regarding infant care, feeding and infant behavior was also stated as important areas where information was needed.

103. Burden, R.L.
     1980 "Measuring the Effects of Stress on
     the Mothers of Handicapped Infants:
     Must Depression Always Follow." CHILD
     CARE HEALTH DEV. 6(2):111-125.

104. Burgi, V.S.
     1954 "Puerperalpsychose oder
     diencephalosis Puerperalis?" SCHWEIZ.
     MED. WCHNSCHR. 84:1224-1225.

105. Burrows, Graham D.; Trevor R. Norman; and
     Brian M. Davies.
     1983 "Psychiatric Disorders in the
     Puerperium." In: HANDBOOK OF
     PSYCHOSOMATIC OBSTETRICS AND
     GYNAECOLOGY. (Dennerstein and Burrows,
     Eds.) Elsevier Biomedical Press. pp.
     309-336.

     1) Summary. 4) Separated into: a)
     Postpartum dysphorias--weepiness, usually
     days 1-10, lability, "blues", feeling
     miserable; b) postnatal
     depression--usually develops around third
     week puerperium or after, varies in
     intensity, worsens as day progresses,
     reactive to circumstances, fatigue,
     irritability, sleep disturbance,
     difficulty in normal household chores,
     problems with partner; c) Puerperal
     psychoses--postpartum schizophrenia,
     manic-depressive psychosis or toxic
     exhaustive psychosis. 7) Treatment
     depends on severity and whether or not
     symptoms are associated with another
     well-defined illness. Suggests severe
     depressive episodes treated with ECT where
     pharmacotherapy is unsuccessful. Mild
     episodes receive psychotherapy and
     benzodiazepine. Moderate to severe

usually receive antidepressant drugs.

106. Burton, J.L.
1974 "Prolactin and Depression." LANCET
1(845):26.

107. Butts, H.F.
1969 "Postpartum Psychiatric Problems, a
Review of the Literature Dealing with
Etiological Theories." J. NATL. MED.
ASSOC. 61(2):136-139.

108. Calcedo Ordonez, A., et al.
1975 "Puerperal Psychoses (Catamaestic and
Clinical Studies of 20 Cases)." ACTA
LUSO ESP. NEUROL. PSIGUIATRIC
3(4):209-230. (Eng. Abstr).

109. Cammer, Leonard.
1969 "The Exhaustion of Adaptive Reserve
and Depression." DIS. NERV. SYSTEM
SUPPL. 30(2):131-133.

110. Caplan, G.
1957 "Psychological Aspects of Maternity
Care." AM. J. PUBLIC HEALTH 45:25-31.

111. Carnes, J.W.
1983 "Psycho-social Disturbances During
and After Pregnancy - Helping the
Patient Cope with Prenatal Stress and
Postpartum Blues." POSTGR. MED.
73(1):135.

112. Carroll, Bernard J., and Meir Steiner.
1978 "The Psychobiology of Premenstrual
Dysphoria: The Role of Prolactin."
PSYCHONEUROENDOCRIN. 3(2):171-180.

24

113. Chalmers, I., et al.
     1979 PERINATAL MEDICINE: SIXTH EUROPEAN
     CONGRESS. Stuttgart: Geog Thiene.

114. Chapman, A.H.
     1959 "Obsessions of Infanticide." AM. MED.
     ASSOC. ARCH. GEN. PSYCHIAT. 1:28-32.

115. Chertok, L.
     1972 "The Psychopathology of Vomiting of
     Pregnancy." In: MODERN PERSPECTIVES IN
     PSYCHO-OBSTETRICS. (J.G. Howells, Ed.)
     New York: Brunner/Mazel.

116. Christian, E.P.
     1889 "What Is Puerperal Mania, and What
     Constitutes Puerperal Insanity?" ANN.
     GYNAEC. 2:449-457.

117. Churchill, F.
     1850 "On the Mental Disorders of Pregnancy
     and Childbirth." AM. J. INSAN.
     7:297-317.

118. Clark, Margaret.
     1970 HEALTH IN THE MEXICAN-AMERICAN
     CULTURE. Berkeley and Los Angeles:
     University of California Press.

119. Clarke, Geoffrey.
     1913 "The Forms of Mental Disorder
     Occurring in Connection with
     Childbearing." J. MENT. SCI. 59:67.

120. Clarke, Michael, and Antony J. Williams.
     1979 "Depression in Women After Perinatal
     Death." LANCET 8122:916-917.

121. Clements, Marcelle.
     1980 "The Mid-Life Maternity Blues." NEW
        YORK, September 8, pp. 34-48.

122. Close, Sylvia.
     1980 BIRTH REPORT: EXTRACTS FROM OVER
        4,000 PERSONAL EXPERIENCES. Windsor,
        Berks: Nfer Publishing Co., Ltd.

     1) Descriptive. 6) "Many women (but not
     all) experience 'post-natal blues' after
     the delivery. This is characterized by
     spells of weepiness--starts three to five
     days after the baby is born and usually
     only lasts for a short time. The best
     treatment is extra affection and
     understanding from the husband, and
     encouraging help with the baby."

123. Cogan, R., and J.C. Winer.
     1982 "Effects of Childbirth Education
        Communication-Skills Training on
        Postpartum Reports of Parents." BIRTH
        9(4):241-244.

124. Cohen, N.W.
     1977 "Minimizing Emotional Sequellae of
        Cesarean Childbirth." BIRTH FAMILY J.
        4(3):114-119.

125. Collomb, H.; R. Guena; and B. Diop.
     1972 "Psychological and Social Factors in
        the Pathology of Childbearing."
        PSYCHIATRY 1(1):77-89.

126. Colman, Arthur D.
     1969 "Psychological State During First
        Pregnancy." AM. J. ORTHOPSYCHIAT.
        39:788-797.

127. Conolly, J.
     1846 "Description and Treatment of
     Puerperal Insanity." LANCET 1:349-354.

128. Conrad, K.
     1960 "Die Symptomatischen Psychosen." In:
     PSYCHIATRIE DE GENENWART. Volume II.
     Berlin: Springer. pp. 369-453.

129. Cookson, J.C.
     1982 "Postpartum Mania, Dapamine, and
     Estrogens." LANCET 2(8299):672.

130. Cooper, B., and H.G. Morgan.
     1973 "Childbirth and Mental Illness." In:
     EPIDEMIOLOGICAL PSYCHIATRY. Springfield:
     Thomas.

131. Cosminsky, S.
     1977 "Childbirth and Midwifery on a
     Guatemalan Finca." MED. ANTHROP.
     1:69-104.

132. COWLES, C.
     1906 "Is Childbearing a Cause of Mental
     Disease?" BOSTON SOC. PSYCHIAT.
     12:788-791.

133. Cox, John L.
     1976 "Psychiatric Morbidity and
     Childbirth: A Prospective Study from
     Kasangati Health Center, Kampala."
     PROC. ROY. SOC. MED. 69(3):221-222.

134. _____.
1978 "Psychiatric Morbidity and
Childbearing: A Study of 263 Semi-Rural
Ugandan Women." D.M. Thesis, Oxford
University.

135. _____.
1983 "Postnatal Depression - A Comparison
of African and Scottish Women." SOC.
PSYCH. 18(1):25-28.

136. _____.
1978 "Some Socio-Cultural Determinants of
Psychiatric Morbidity Associated with
Childbearing." In: MENTAL ILLNESS IN
PREGNANCY AND THE PUERPERIUM. (Sandler,
Meiton, eds.) London: Oxford
University Press. pp. 91-97.

1) Prospective. 2) 263 Pregnant Ugandan
women, who had attended an antenatal
clinic at a semi-rural health clinic as
well as 89 nonpregnant and nonpuerperal
women were interviewed. 3) A
questionnaire was administered to these
women and if possible a second interview
was administered later. 5) Standardized
Interview Schedule (SIS). 6) One main
finding of the study is that the
"colonial" hypothesis that childbearing in
African women is "natural" and
trouble-free has received no support. And
the frequency of puerperal depression was
comparable with that found in London
women. These findings seem to contradict
his study on Ugandan women in 1979.

137. _____ .
    1979 "A Ugandan Puerperal Psychosis." SOC.
    PSYCHIAT. 14(1):49-52.

    1) Prospective. 2) The sample consisted
    of 31 women who attended the ante- and
    postnatal clinics at Kasangati Teaching
    Health Center, ten miles from Kampala.
    Cohorts were not selected other than by
    their willingness to be interviewed. The
    greater portion of the sample worked at
    home with traditional tasks of
    child-rearing, cultivating, and cooking.
    3) Twenty pilot interviews were conducted
    to establish the range of beliefs
    concerning "amakiro," the traditional
    puerperal illness. The subsequent
    semi-structured interviews enquired
    systematically about the onset, the
    etiology, symptoms, and treatment of the
    illness. All interviews were conducted by
    a native-born medical student (male) in
    the vernacular. A European-born
    researcher (female) assisted. 5) The
    concept "amakiro" developed as a result of
    the interviews; see below. 6) Ninety
    percent state they had heard of "amakiro,"
    78.5% described the symptom of wanting to
    eat the baby, and 60.6% said mental
    confusion would also occur. Sixty and
    six-tenths percent thought the illness
    occured shortly after delivery. Among
    others, 53% thought the illness to be
    caused by the non-use of herbal baths and
    50% to the promiscuity of pregnant women.
    Author discussed his reservations
    concerning the identification of "amakiro"
    with the western concept of postpartum
    depression and stated "Only a detailed
    study of women with 'amakiro' could
    elucidate further whether this belief

could be regarded as a symptom of a
depressive illness or of another major
psychosis."

138. Cox, John L., et al.
    1983 "Prospective Study of the Psychiatric
    Disorders of Childbirth by Self Report
    Questionnaire." J. AFFECT. DISORDERS
    5:1-7.

1) Prospective. 2) 425 Women from
Edinburgh who had attended any one of four
antenatal clinics between January and
October 1978 were included. Of those, 230
completed two scales on four occasions.
3) Two self report questionnaires were
used: The Anxiety and Depression
questionnaire (SAD) and a series of ten
Visual Analysis Scales (VAS) of the
authors' own design. 4) The SAD has two
subscales--anxiety and depression. The
VAS measured feelings of anxiety,
depression, tears, lability, panic,
irritability, fatigue, uselessness,
happiness and calmness. 5) See #3. 6) No
significant changes in mean scores on
anxiety and depression subscales of the
SAD amoung the four occasions. The VAS
scores showed a significant increase in
scores of anxiety, depression, and tears
between 23rd week of pregnancy and 1st
week postpartum, and a significant
decrease in the same scales' scores 1st
week postpartum.

139. Cox, J.L.; Y.M. Connor; I. Henderson; R.J.
     McGuire; and R.E. Kendell.
     1983 "Prospective Study of the
     Pyschiatric-Disorders of Childbirth by
     Self Report Questionaire." J. AFFECT.
     DIS. 5(1):1-7.

140. Crandon, A.J.
     1979 "Maternal Anxiety and Neonatal
     Wellbeing." J. PSYCHOSOM. RES.
     23:113-115.

141. Crnic, K.A., et al.
     1984 "Maternal Stress and Social Support -
     Effects on the Mother - and Infant
     Relationship from Birth to 18 Months."
     AM. J. ORTHOP. 54(2):224-235.

142. Cruickshank, W.H.
     1940 "Psychosis Associated With Pregnancy
     and the Puerperium." CANADIAN MED.
     ASSOC. J. 43:571-576.

143. Cutrona, Carolyn E.
     1982 "Nonpsychotic Postpartum Depression:
     A Review of Recent Research." CLINICAL
     PSYCHOLOGY REVIEW 2(4):487-503.

     1) Summary. 4) Symptoms include:
     Depression and anxiety that persist beyond
     the first week postpartum and interferes t
     some extent with the woman's ability to
     function, irritability, insomnia, guilt,
     and feelings of inadequacy. 6) Suggests
     that prolonged postpartum depression is
     closely linked to stressful events around
     the time of pregnancy and delivery, and a
     lack of social support. Recommends
     further research that recognizes the
     interplay of environmental, psychological,
     and physiological variables.

144. _____.
1983 "Causal Attributions and Perinatal
Depression." J. ABNORMAL PSYCHOL.
92(2):161-172.

1) Prospective. 2) 85 third trimester
first-time mothers recruited through
obstetrics clinics, Lamaze classes, and a
community newspaper. 3) Three interviews:
First during third trimester, then 2 weeks
postpartum, and 8 weeks postpartum using 6
scales. 5) Beck Diagnostic Inventory and
the Hamilton Rating Scale for Depression.
6) Pregnancy scores on the ASQ did predict
level of postpartum depression among women
not depressed during pregnancy, but not
among women who were depressed during
pregnancy. Speed of recovery from
symptoms was significantly predicted by
attributional style.

145. Dalton, Katharina.
1971 "Prospective Study Into Puerperal
Depression." BR. J. PSYCHIATRY
118(547):689-692.

146. _____.
1971 "Puerperal and Premenstrual
Depression." PROC. R. SOC. MED.
64(12):1249-1252.

147. _____.
1980 DEPRESSION AFTER CHILDBIRTH. Oxford:
Oxford University Press.

148. Daly, K.J.
     1967 "Psychosis Associated with the Use of
     a Sequential Oral Contraceptive."
     LANCET 2:444-445.

149. Daly, Michael J.
     1975 "Psychological Impact of Surgical
     Procedures on Women." In:
     COMPREHENSIVE TEXTBOOK OF PSYCHIATRY.
     (A.M. Freedman, H.I. Kaplan, and B.J.
     Sadock, eds.) Volume 2, 2nd edition.
     Baltimore: Williams and Wilkins. pp.
     1477-1480.

150. Daniels, R.S., and H. Lessow.
     1964 "Severe Postpartum Reactions: An
     Interpersonal View." PSYCHOSOMAT.
     5:21-26.

151. Danowski, T.S., et al.
     1953 "Is Pregnancy Followed by Relative
     Hypothyroidism?" AM. J. OBSTET. GYNEC.
     65:77-80.

152. Dargis, Jurate J.
     1978 "Postpartum Adjustment and Exercise."
     DISS. ABSTR. INTL. 38(11-b):5634.

153. Davenport, Y.B., and M.L. Adland.
     1982 "Postpartum Psychoses in Female and
     Male Bipolar Manic-Depressive Parents."
     AM. J. ORTHOP. 52(2):288-297.

154. David, H.P.
     1983 "Postpartum and Post Abortion
     Mental-Health in Denmark." FAMILY PLAN.
     PE. 15(4):156

155. Davidson, G.M.
1936 "Concerning Schizophrenia and
Manic-Depressive Psychoses Associated
with Pregnancy and Childbirth." AM. J.
PSYCHIAT. 92:1331-1346.

156. Davidson, J.R.T.
1972 "Post-partum Mood Change in Jamaican
Women: A Description and Discussion on
Its Significance." BR. J. PSYCHIAT.
121(565):659-663.

1) Prospective. 2) Fifty-five women
referred to the antenatal clinic of the
University of the West Indies, Kingston,
participated in the study. All cohorts
were residents of Kingston. 3) Tests were
administered at 14-18 weeks and repeated
at 30-34 weeks prepartum. Postpartum
interviews were conducted daily at which
time a Beck Depression Inventory was
completed, a record made of any crying,
and in a semi-structured manner questions
were asked about feelings towards the
infant, feeding difficulties, doubts about
individual's capacity to cope as a mother,
and worries regarding home, money, etc.
4) Birth to 11 days, inclusive, was
defined as the postpartum period. 5) Beck
Depression Inventory; Taylor Manifest
Anxiety Scale; a subjectively based rating
scale for the "blues" was chosen: a) No
blues--no episodes of crying or sad
feelings; b) Mild blues--less than 3
crying episodes, or less than 3 sad days
reported or a combination of both; and c)
Severe blues--More than 2 crying episodes,
or more than 2 sad days or a combination
of both. 6) The racial composition of the
group was 40 Negro and 3 Indian. The age
distribution was from 17 to 38, with a

mean of 25.1 years. Distribution of parity was: Primiparae, 19; Multiparae (2-4), 10; and Grande Multiparae (5-9), 14. Altogether, 60.4% reported one or more episodes of the blues during the first 11 days postpartum, mostly days one, two, and three. The variables with which the blues held a statistically significant relationship were: Multiparity, frequency of tubal ligation, negative attitudes during pregnancy, higher Taylor Manifest Anxiety Scores in the first trimester, and higher Beck Depression Inventory Scores postpartum. No statistical relationship was demonstrated with other obstetric factors, postpartum complications, neonatal state, breast-feeding problems, desired sex of the child, age, marital status, and family and past patient history of psychiatric illness. Author does caution that "In this particular group, there was much Iron Deficiency Anaemia, and this could have been a contributor; the same could be said for Folate lack in a population where malnutrition is widespread."

157. Daysh, E.S.
    1973 "Nursing Care Study: Puerperal Psychosis." NURS. MIRROR 137(7): 43-44.

158. de Anda, Diane, and R.M. Bercerra.
    1984 "Support Networks for Adolescent Mothers." SOC. CASE 65(3):172-181.

159. Dean, C., and R.E. Kendell.
    1981 "The Symptomatology of Puerperal Illness." BR. J. PSYCHIAT. 139:128-133.

160. Delay, Jean, et al.
1948 "Explorations cyto-hormonales aucours
des psychoses du post-partum." ANN.
MED. PSYCHOL. 106(1):62-69.

161. _____.
1953 "Traitement des psychoses du post
partum." ANN. ENDOCR. 14:428-431.

162. Deutsch, H.
1945 MOTHERHOOD. VOLUME 2. New York; Grune
and Stratton.

163. _____.
1945 THE PSYCHOLOGY OF WOMAN. VOLUMES I
AND II. New York: Grune and Stratton.

164. Devore, N.E.
1979 "The Relationship Between Previous
Elective Abortions and Postpartum
Depressive Reactions." JOGN.
8(4):237-240.

165. Dingley, E.F.
1979 "Birthplace and Attendants: Oregon's
Alternative Experience." WOMEN AND
HEALTH 4(3):239-254.

166. Doering, S.G., and D.R. Entwisle.
1975 "Preparation During Pregnancy and
Ability to Cope with Labor and
Delivery." AM. J. ORTHOPSYCHIAT.
45:825-837.

167. Donaldson, Nancy E.
1977 "Fourth Trimester Follow-up." AM. J.
NURS. 77(7):1176-1178.

1) Summary. 7) Suggests an examination of
all postpartum mothers for any signs of
complications. An example is given of a

program at Hoag Memorial
Hospital--Presbyterian, Newport Beach, CA.
This postpartum program entails a
maternity nursing unit telephoning new
mothers in the hospital, then 3 to 7 days
after returning home and inquiring their
condition. The results are then given to
the appropriate medical staff and
assessed. When needed, the patients are
referred to community resources. (by
comparison, see Robertson, 1980 for
Canada's revolutionary self-help program).

168. Donelda, J.E., and Roberta Hewat.
     1985 "Mother's Postpartum Perceptions of
        Spousal Relationships." JOGN.
        14(2):140-46.

     1) Prospective. 2) 194 mothers registered
     to give birth in a large urban hospital.
     3) Self-administered rating scales and
     open-ended questions at one, three and six
     months postpartum. 6) This study
     corroborates the findings of others
     concerning postpartum sexuality. Libido
     and enjoyment declined more for women than
     men. At five months the "emotional
     closeness" of the parental relationship
     increased for 20%, decreased for 47%, and
     remained the same for 33%. 7) Information
     and support for parents before and after
     birth regarding sexuality is encouraged.

169. Dorzhadamba, S.
     1965 "The Epidemiology of Mental Illness
        in the Mongolian People's Republic."
        TRANSCULTURAL PSYCHIATRIC RESEARCH
        REVIEW 2:19-22.

170. Douglas, G.
     1956 "Psychotic Mothers." LANCET
     1:124-125.

171. _____.
     1963 "Puerperal Depression and Excessive
     Compliance with the Mother." BR. J.
     MED. PSYCHOL. 36:271-278.

172. _____.
     1968 "Some Emotional Disorders of the
     Puerperium." J. PSYCHOSOM. RES.
     12:101-106.

173. Dowling, Scott.
     1980 "Going Forth to Meet the Environment:
     A Developmental Study of Seven Infants
     with Esophageal Atresia." PSYCHOSOM.
     MED. 42(suppl. 1:II):153-161.

174. Ebie, J.C.
     1972 "Psychiatric Illness in the
     Puerperium Among Nigerians." TROP.
     GEOGR. MED. 24:253-256.

1) Retrospective. 2) All patients who
were diagnosed as suffering from
psychiatric illness in the puerperium on
admission to the University College
Hospital, Ibadan, from 1960 to 1969 were
identified as the study population. Data
is concerned with 55 of the original 61
cases. 4) The puerperium was defined as
the first six weeks following delivery.
5) Author relied on the diagnosis of the
attending physician. 6) Sixteen patients
were diagnosed as schizophrenic, seven of
which were catatonic, 14 as confusional
state, ten as affective disorder, seven as
unspecified, four as schizo-affective
disorder, and four as neurotic.

Thirty-six patients had a febrile illness
in the puerperium; this illness occured
before or coincided with the onset of
their psychiatric symptoms. Twenty-three
patients had other physical illnesses and
31 had none. Four of the 58 patients died
in hospital. Thirty-three of the cases
had delivered in the hospital, nine had
delivered in other medical or maternity
centers, while 16 delivered elsewhere.

175. Eichholz, Alice.
     1980 "A Psychohistorical View of 19th and
     20th Century Birth Practices." In:
     PSYCHOLOGICAL ASPECTS OF PREGNANCY,
     BIRTHING, AND BONDING. (Barbara L.
     Blum, ed.) New York: Human Sciences
     Press. pp. 249-256.

176. Engelhard, J.L.B.
     1912 "On Puerperal Psychoses and the
     Influence of Gestation Period on
     Psychiatric and Neurological Disease
     Already in Existence." Z. GEBURTSCH.
     GYNAK. 70, 727. -374.

177. Engelmann, George J.
     1977 LABOR AMOUNG PRIMITIVE PEOPLES,
     SHOWING THE DEVELOPMENT OF THE OBSTETRIC
     SCIENCE OF TODAY, FROM THE NATURAL AND
     INSTINCTIVE CUSTOMS OF ALL RACES,
     CIVILIZED AND SAVAGE, PAST AND PRESENT.
     (Originally published 1882) New York:
     AMS Press.

1) Descriptive survey. 2) Author's
personal observation of traditional
cultures globally (1882) 6) Descriptive
account of the activities surrounding
childbirth. Focus is primarily on the
various positions employed during

parturition, however, there is some
mention of care in the early postpartum.
Author makes no mention of postpartum
depression, per se, but does state "...of
milk fever they seem to know nothing"
(p.XVIII). This remark is significant
when one notes the date of publication.
Due to the relationship between strange
behavior and the onset of lactation as
late as 1880 postpartum problems were
still generally viewed as internal
physiological problems and in europe the
condition was described as milk fever.
Therefore, one is not certain if the
author was referring to the physiological
or the psychological problem.

178. Englert, E.H.
     1974 "Subconscious Anxiety About Children as
     Cause of Pains in Pregnancy and Postpartum
     Depression with Presentation of 12 Cases."
     ZEITSCHRIGT FUR KLINISCHE PSYCHOLOGIE UND
     PSYCOTHERAPIE 22(1):88-90.

179. Esquirol, J.E.D.
     1838 "Des maladies mentales considerees sous
     les rapports medical." VOLUME I.   In:
     HYGIENIQUE ET MEDICO-LEGAL. Paris:
     Bailliere.

180. Evans, P.
     1968 "Infanticide." PROC. ROY. SOC. MED.
     61:36-68.

181. Falls, Frederick Howard, and Charlotte
     Sinclair Holt.
     1961 ATLAS OF OBSTETRIC COMPLICATIONS.
     Philadelphia: J.B. Lippincott.

182. Feinstein, A.F.
     1964 "Group Therapy for Mothers With
          Infanticide Impulses." AM. J. PSYCHIAT.
          120:882.

183. Feldman, F., et al.
     1946 "Shock Treatment of Psychoses
          Associated with Pregnancy." J. NERV. &
          MENT. DIS. 103:494-502.

184. Fink, Robert M.
     1979 "Prepartum and Postpartum Depression:
          The Psychological Concomitants." DISS.
          ABSTR. INTL. 39(7-B):3509-3510S.

185. Fishback, D.
     1939 "Mental Illness Associated with
          Child-bearing." ELGIN STATE HOSPITAL
          PAPERS 3:156-165.

186. Flamholtz-Trien, S.
     1977 "Chasing Those Blues Away." AM. BABY
          39(5):26, 39.

187. Ford, C.S.
     1945 A COMPARATIVE STUDY OF HUMAN
          REPRODUCTION. New Haven: Yale University
          Press.

188. Foundeur, Marvin; Carl Fixsen; William A.
     Triebel; and Mary Alice White.
     1957 "Postpartum Mental Illness: Controlled
          Study." A. ARCH. NEUROL. & PSYCHIAT.
          77(5):503-512.

189. Frake, Charles O., and Carolyn M. Frake.
     1957 "Post-Natal Care Among the Eastern
          Subanum." SILLIMAN JOURNAL 4:207-215.

190. Frate, Dennis A.; Joel B. Cowen; Allison H.
Rutledge; and Michael Glasser.
1979 "Behavioral Reactions During the
Postpartum Period: Experiences of 108
Women." WOMEN & HEALTH 4(4):355-371.

1) Retrospective. 2) 108 Postpartum women
were selected from newspaper notices. 3)
Data were collected in this study through
the use of a mailed survey. 4) Postpartum
depression was defined as particular
behavioral responses apparently related to
the birth processes which occur up to one
year postpartum. 5) Zung Self Rating
Depression Scale. 6) Significant
relationship found between postpartum
depression and mother's age and amount of
assistance by spouse in the home. In
addition, prior expectations and spread
between oldest and youngest child related
to depression.

191. Freeman, Thomas.
1951 "Pregnancy as a Precipitant of Mental
Illness in Men." BR. J. MED. PSYCHOL.
14:49-54.

192. Fried, M.N., and M.H. Fried.
1980 TRANSITIONS: FOUR RITUALS IN EIGHT
CULTURES. New York: Norton.

1) Ethnography. 6) Case studies of Kung
(Africa, Kalahari Desert), Tikopia (New
Hebrides), Tlingit (Alaska), Muclim Hausa
(Nigeria), and Taiwan cultures were
received for data relating to birth. The
descriptions of birth in Taiwan is the
most useful regarding the postpartum
period as the others quickly move to
childrearing. In Taiwan, tso yueh, or "do
the month" is practiced and can be traced

to the 10th century. This ritual involves
30 days of complete rest. The new mother
is not allowed to wash her hair, body,
dishes, or clothes; she must avoid cold
water. If this rule is broken wind will
enter through joints and apertures and
cause chronic asthma and arthritis. She
must avoid raw or cold food, i.e. turnips,
cabbage, leafy green vegetables and most
fruits. Duck and fish, and salt, also are
avoided. Prefered foods are "hot," i.e.
chicken cooked in sesame oil and wine.
After 30 days the man yueh ceremony is
held where the baby is introduced to
relatives and neighbors and the child's
name is announced. During the tso yueh,
the mother is seen as vulnerable and is
provided great physical and emotional
support.

193. Fries, M.
     1944 "Psychosomatic Relationships Between
     Mother and Infant." PSYCHOSOM. MED.
     6:159.

194. Frommer, Eva A., and Gillian O'Shea.
     1973 "Antenatal Identification of Women
     Liable to Have Problems in Managing
     Their Infants." BR. J. PSYCHIAT.
     123:149-156.

195. _____.
     1973 "The Importance of Childhood
     Experience in Relation to Problems of
     Marriage and Family-Building." BR. J.
     PSYCHIAT. 123:157-160.

196. Frumkes, G.
     1934 "Mental Disorders Related to
          Childbirth." J. NERV. & MENT. DIS.
          79:540-552.

197. Furstner, C.
     1875 "Ueber Schwangerschafts- And
          Puerperalpsychosen." ARCH. PSYCHIAT.
          5:505-543.

198. Gardiner, A.; N. Porteous; and J.A.
     Walker-Smith.
     1972 "The Effect of Coeliac Disease on the
          Mother-Child Relationship." AUST. J.
          8(1):39-43.

199. Garner, A., and C. Wenar.
     1959 THE MOTHER CHILD INTERACTION IN
          PSYCHOSOMATIC DISORDERS. Urbana:
          University of Illinois Press.

200. Gartner, Dorothy, and Harris S. Goldstein.
     1972 "Some Characteristics of Mothers of
          Severely Disturbed Children in a
          Therapeutic Nursery." PSYCHOL. REPORTS
          30(3):901-902.

201. Garvey, Michael J., and Gary D. Tollefson.
     1984 "Postpartum Depression." J. OF REPRO.
          MED. 29(2):113-116.

1) Summary. 4) Symptoms most common are:
dysphoria, appetite or weight change,
insomnia or hypersomnia, psychomotor
agitation or retardation, loss of interest
or pleasure in usual activities, loss of
energy, feelings of worthlessness or
guilt, difficulty concentrating,
remembering or making decisions and/or
thoughts of death or suicide that are
present daily for two or more weeks. 7)

Drug therapy--antidepressants are claimed
to be useful. Cognitive or interpersonal
therapy may be effective in some
depressive disorders.

202. Garvey, M.J., and R. Tollefso.
     1984 "Postpartum Depression." J. REPRO.
     MED. 29(3):113-116.

203. Garvey, M.J.; V.B. Tuason; A.E. Lumry; and
     N.G. Hoffmann.
     1983 "Occurrence of Depression in the
     Postpartum State." J. AFFECT. DISORDERS
     5(2):97-101.

1) Retrospective. 2) 54 women. 17 were
postpartum depressives with recurrent
affective disorder and 37 with children
and recurrent affective disorder, but no
postpartum depression. 3) Comparisons
were made among the selected women using
multiple variables of illness.
Statistically Significant Paired T-Test
was applied. 4) Postpartum depression is
a depression starting within 2 months of
parturition. 5) RDC diagnosis of major
depressive disorder or mania. 6) Data
support proposition that depression is
more common in the postpartum period than
would be expected by chance alone. Once a
postpartum depression has occurred, the
incidence of future episodes following
pregnancy is substantial, approximately
75% higher.

204. Gath, Ann.
     1977 "Emotional Needs in a New Family."
     NURS. MIRROR AND MIDWIFES J.
     143(28):52-54.

205. Gazella, J.G.
     1981 "Baby Blues - Causes and Cures." BABY
     TALK. 46:5.

206. Gelder, M.
     1978 "Hormones and Post-partum
     Depression." In: MENTAL ILLNESS IN
     PREGNANCY AND THE PUERPERIUM. (M.
     Sandler, ed.) London: Oxford University
     Press.

207. Giaquinto, S.; F. Marciano; and G. Nolfe.
     1979 "Alpha Increase in Puerperium."
     ELECTROENCEPHALOGR. CLIN. NEUROPHYSIOL.
     46(2):197-204.

1) Prospective. 2) 17 primiparas were
compared to a control group of 16
nonpregnant women of the same age range.
3) EEG's were recorded three times on the
pregnant women: a) At the 32nd week of
pregnancy, b) 48-72 hours after delivery,
c) and 15 days later. Prolactin level
tested 3 times: a) 32nd week, b) 36th
week, c) and 72 hours after delivery. The
control group, however, was recorded 2
times at a 24-hour interval. 6) An alpha
increase was observed from the 32nd week
of pregnancy to 48-72 hours after
delivery. In 47% of the cases a
significant increase was observed in most
critical regions. Experience of
relaxation and feelings of quietness were
commonly found in the first days after
delivery. An obvious prolactin level
increase was found during pregnancy.
Blocking of lactation left the alpha
activity unchanged.

208. Gideon, Helen.
     1962 "A Baby is Born in the Punjab." AM.
     ANTHRO. 64:1220-1234.

209. Ginath, Y.
     1974 "Psychoses in Males in Relation to
     Their Wives' Pregnancy and Childbirth."
     ISS. ANN. PSYCHIAT. 12:227-237.

210. Godding, W.W.
     1874 "Puerperal Insanity." BOSTON M. & S.
     J. 91:317-319.

211. Goddwin, J.; J. Goddwin; and G. Chance.
     1976 PERINATAL MEDICINE. Baltimore:
     Williams & Wilkins.

212. Goldstein, H.H.; J. Weinberg; and M.I.
     Sankstone.
     1941 "Shock Therapy in Psychosis
     Complicating Pregnancy. A Case Report."
     AM. J. PSYCHIAT. 98:201-202.

213. Gordon, Richard E.
     1957 "Emotional Disorders of Pregnancy and
     Childbearing." J. M. SOC. NEW JERSEY
     54:16.

214. _____.
     1961 THE PREVENTION OF POSTPARTUM
     EMOTIONAL DIFFICULTIES. Ann Arbor,
     Michigan: University Microfilms.

215. Gordon, Richard E., and Katherine K.
     Gordon.
     1959 "Prediction and Treatment of
     Emotional Disorders of Pregnancy and
     Childbearing." AM. J. OBSTET. GYNEC.
     77:1074.

216. _____.
1960 "Social Factors in the Prevention of
Postpartum Emotional Difficulties."
OBSTET. GYNEC. 15:433.

217. _____.
1967 "Factors in Postpartum Emotional
Adjustment." AM. J. ORTHOPSYCHIAT.
37:359-360.

218. Gordon, Richard E.; Katherine K. Gordon;
and Eli E. Kapostins.
1965 "Factors in Postpartum Emotional
Adjustment." OBSTETRICS AND GYNECOLOGY
25(2):158-166.

219. Goshen-Gottstein, E.R.
1966 MARRIAGE AND FIRST PREGNANCY:
CULTURAL INFLUENCES ON ATTITUDES OF
ISRAELI WOMEN. London: Tavistock.

220. Grace, Jeanne T.
1978 "Good Grief: Coming to Terms with the
Childbirth Experience." JOGN.
7(1):18-24.

221. Granquist, H.N.
1947 BIRTH AND CHILDHOOD AMOUNG THE ARABS:
STUDIES IN A MUHAMMEDAN VILLAGE IN
PALESTINE. Helsingfors: Soderstrom.

222. Grecu, G.H., et al.
1975 "Clinico-Statistical Observations on
Puerperal Psychosyndromes." REV. MED.
INTERN (NEUROL. PSYCHIAT.) 20(4):297-303.
(ENG. ABSTR.)

223. Greengrass, P.M., and S.R. Tonge.
1972 "Brain Monoamine Metabolism in the
Mouse During the Immediate Post-partum
Period." BR. PHARMACOL. SOC. 533.

224. Griest, Douglas; Karen C. Wells; and Rex
     Forehand.
     1979 "An Examination of Predictors of
     Maternal Perceptions of Maladjustment in
     Clinic-Referred Children." J. ABNORMAL
     PSYCHOL. 88(3):277-281.

225. Grimmel, K., and V.L. Larsen.
     1965 "Postpartum and Depressive
     Psychiatric Symptoms and Thyroid
     Activity." J. AM. MED. ASSOC.
     20(6):542-546.

226. Grossman, Frances K., et al.
     1980 PREGNANCY, BIRTH, AND PARENTING:
     ADOPTATION OF MOTHERS, FATHERS &
     INFANTS. San Francisco: Jossey-Bass.

227. Grubb, C.
     1980 "Perceptions of Time by Multiparous
     Women in Relation to Themselves and
     Others During the First Postpartal
     Month." MATERN. CHILD NURS. J.
     9(4):225-331.

228. Gruis, M.
     1977 "Beyond Maternity: Postpartum
     Concerns of Mothers." AM. J. MATERN.
     CHILD. NURS. 2(3):182-188.

229. Grundy, P.F., and C.J. Roberts.
     1975 "Observations on the Epidemiology of
     Postpartum Mental Illness." PSYCHOL.
     MED. 5(3):286-290.

     1) Retrospective. 2) All consecutive
     maternal residents of Cardiff from 1965 to
     1972, inclusive, were reviewed. Data was
     extracted from the Cardiff birth survey.
     Sixty-seven cases of postpartum mental
     illness were found from 35,486

confinements during the specified period.
3) Information was compared with that
obtained for the total Cardiff resident
confinements for the same period who acted
as controls. 4) Birth to twenty-eight
days was defined as the postpartum period.
5) Author relied on the diagnosis of the
attending physician. 6) The incidence of
postpartum mental illness was found to be
1.9 per thousand births. Sixty-three
percent of the affected women conceived
during October to March, inclusive. The
mean age of the cases was 28.4 years
compared with 26.2 for controls. No
significant difference was found between
cases and controls in respect to social
class, parity, weight gain, and
gestational age, birth weight, and sex of
infant.

230. Grunebaum, Henry, and J. Weiss.
1963 "Psychotic Mothers and Their
Children: Joint Admission to an Adult
Psychiatric Hospital." AM. J. PSYCHIAT.
119:927-933.

231. Grunebaum, Henry; Bertram J. Cohler; Carol
Kauffman; and David Gallant.
1978 "Children of Depressed and
Schizophrenic Mothers." CHILD PSYCHIAT.
AND HUMAN DEV. 8(4):219-228.

232. Gundry, R.
1859 "Observations upon Puerperal
Insanity." AM. J. INSAN. 16:294-320.

233. Gunter, Nancy C., and Richard C. Labarba.
1981 "Maternal and Perinatal Effects on
Adolescent Childbearing." INT. J.
BEHAVIORAL DEV. 4:333-357.

1) Prospective, with an excellent summary.
2) 60 pregnant adolescents (aged 14-17)
and 60 pregnant adults as a control group
(aged 20-29). Subjects were obtained from
a public health department clinic and were
in the last days of the first trimester or
in the second trimester. Both the study
and control groups were low income; 23%
black multiparas, 3% white multiparas.
90% of blacks unmarried, 42% of whites
unmarried. 3) They all received
multivitamins and iron. Hematocrit levels
were taken at every visit so iron dosages
could be adjusted as necessary. 5) A
revised state trait anxiety inventory
along with the multiple affect adjective
checklist and a variety of biological
variables were recorded. 6) No
significant differences were found in the
groups according to maternal and infant
complications. Higher levels of
depression, anxiety, and hostility were
found in the antepartum as opposed to the
postpartum period. Anxiety in adolescents
did not differ significantly from the
control group. Adolescents and adult
black mothers scored significantly higher
in depression than did the adult white
mothers.

234. Gupta, O.P., et al.
1975 "Psychiatric Illness in the
Puerperium." J. INDIAN MED. ASSOC.
65(2):45-46.

1) Retrospective. 2) All patients

diagnosed as suffering from psychiatric
illness in the puerperium from 1968 to
1973, inclusive, were included in the
study. Thirty-five patients were found
during the period under review. 4) The
postpartum was operationally defined as
birth to six weeks after delivery. 5)
Authors relied on the diagnosis of the
attending physician. 6) Thirty-four of
the 35 patients had been suffering from
anaemia of variable degree and 16 had
febrile illness during the puerperium.
"The large number of confusional states in
this study thus reflects the poor physical
status of the patient" (p. 46). Seven
patients were diagnosed as schizophrenic,
10 as confusional, 8 as affective
disorder, 2 neurotic, and 8 unspecified.
Most of the patients developed psychiatric
symptoms within the first two weeks of
delivery. Twenty-two out of 35 patients
were in the age group of 21-30 years.
Older women did not seem to be
particularly vulnerable. Primiparaes
accounted for the highest number (13 out
of 35) affected. On the average, 6 cases
per year are admitted for puerperal
psychosis.

235. Hagman, A.
1962 "Regression in Puerperal Breakdown."
BR. J. MED. PSYCHOL. 35:135-145.

236. Haire, D.
1973 "The Cultural Warping of Childbirth."
ENVIRONMENTAL CHILD HEALTH 19:171-191.

237. Hakansson Zaunders, Margareta, and Nils
     Uddenberg.
     1975 "Conflicts Regarding Pregnancy and
     the Maternal Role as Reflected in a
     Serial Projective Test Instruments."
     PSYCHOL. RES. BULL. 15(3):15.

238. Halbreich, Uriel, and Jean Endicott.
     1981 "Possible Involvement of Endorphin
     Withdrawal or Imbalance in Specific
     Premenstrual Syndromes and Postpartum
     Depression." MEDICAL HYPOTHESIS
     7:1045-1051.

     1) Commentary. 4) Depressed mood,
     lethargy, anxiety, emotional lability and
     tearfulness in varying degrees of severity
     (described as "neurotic" or "atypical"
     depression). 6) Levels of endorphins and
     estrogen are decreased postpartum. The
     decreased levels of endorphins are related
     to dysphoria, decreased motor activity,
     lability, lethargy and increased sexual
     interest, while increased levels may be
     related to agitation and anxiety.

239. Hallervorden, E.
     1897 "ZUR PATHOGENESE der puerperalen
     NERVENKRANKHEITEN und der toxischen
     PSYCHOSEN." ALLG. ZTSCHR. PSYCHIAT.
     53:661-685.

240. Halonen, Jane Simmons.
     1980 "An Examination of Relaxation
     Training and Expectation Variables in
     the Treatment of Postpartal Distress."
     DISS. ABSTR. INTL. University of
     Wisconsin, Milwaukee. 41(11-B):4263.

241. Hamadah, K.
     1977 "Depression." NURS. MIRROR
     145(19):13-15.

242. Hamburg, D.A.
     1966 "Effects of Progesterone on Human
     Behavior." RES. ASSN. FOR RES. IN NERV.
     MENT. DISEASES 43:251-265.

243. Hamburg, David A.; R.H. Moos; and I.D.
     Yalom.
     1968 "Studies of Distress in the Menstrual
     Cycle and the Postpartum Period." In:
     ENDOCRINOLOGY AND HUMAN BEHAVIOR.
     (Richard P. Michael, ed.) London: Oxford
     University Press. pp. 94-116.

244. Hames, C.J.
     1980 "Sexual Needs and Interests of
     Postpartum Couples." JOGN 9(5):313-335.

245. Hamilton, J.A.
     1962 POSTPARTUM PSYCHIATRIC PROBLEMS. St.
     Louis: C.V. Mosby.

246. Handley, S.L.; T.L. Dunn; J.M. Baker; C.
     Cockshott; and S. Gould.
     1977 "Mood Changes in Puerperium, and
     Plasma Tryptophan and Cortisol
     Concentrations." BR. MED. J. 6078(2):
     18-20.

1) Prospective. 2) United Kingdom-born
women delivering at a maternity unit, aged
18-31, and having live-births were
eligible to participate in the study;
eighteen women participated. 3) A
standard, low-protein breakfast was given
each morning, and drugs known to interfere
with tryptophan binding were avoided.
Samples of venous blood (10 ml) were

obtained daily between 0900 and 0930 and
the plasma was analyzed for cortisol,
total tryptophan, and free tryptophan, The
study was blind in that biochemical
results were not known to the clinician
administering the psychiatric assessment.
4) Postpartum is defined as the second to
fifth day, parturition being regarded as
day 0 of birth. 5) Multiple Affect
Adjective Check List (MAACL); Beck
Depression Inventory; and Hildreth Feeling
Scale. 6) None of the women were
diagnosed as suffering from depression.
Three, however, exhibited slight elevation
of mood (not clinically significant). These
three patients scored significantly lower
for depression and higher for anxiety.
Biochemically the three patients had
unusually high cortisol concentrations on
day 2. Plasma-free tryptophan
concentration showed negative correlation
with MAACL and a positive correlation with
Hildreth scores. Cortisol concentrations
were not related to anxiety nor was there
significant correlation between cortisol
and either free or total tryptophan
concentrations. The concentration of free
tryptophan correlated with total
tryptophan.

247. Hanson, G.D., and M.J. Brown.
     1973 "Waxy Flexibility in a Postpartum
     Woman--A Case Report and Review of the
     Catatonic Syndrome." PSYCHIAT. QUART.
     47:1-9.

248. Harder, W.
     1967 "The Psychopathology of Infanticide."
     ACTA PSYCHIAT. SCAND. 43:196.

249. Harris, Brian.
     1980 "Maternity Blues." BR. J. PSYCHIAT.
     136:520-521.

250. _____.
     1980 "Prospective Trial of L-tryptophan in
     Maternity Blues." BR. J. PSYCHIAT.
     137:233-235.

1) Prospective. 2) 55 subjects, aged
20-35 years, obtained from clinic in 8th
month, multiparous, bottle feeders. 3)
L-tryptophan was given after delivery to
determine whether plasma tryptophan levels
were related to maternity blues. The
control group received placebos. 5) The
drugs were begun within 12 hours of
delivery and continued for 10 days. The
patients were seen daily by the author and
their mental state was assessed according
to the criteria of PITT (1973). A global
assessment of mood change was also made
using the Middlesex Hospital Questionnaire
(MHQ). 6) There was no significant
difference on any pre-delivery data
between the two groups. Also no
significant differences in severity of
mood disorders or tearfulness. Maternity
blues did correlate significantly with
three items on the mhq: anxiety,
depression, and hysteria. Thus, the low
plasma-free tryptophan that correlates
significantly with the degree of mood
change in the puerperium is an
epiphenomenon occurring at the same time
as the blues, but it is not a primary
cause.

251. _____.
1981 "'Maternity Blues' in East African
Clinic Attenders." ARCH. GEN. PSYCHIAT.
38(11):1293-1295.

1) Retrospective. 2) 50 East African
mothers seen at health center in Dar Es
Salaam, Tanzania, within 2 to 16 weeks
after delivery. 3) Structured 60-minute
interview which included: a) Obtaining
data concerning the pregnancy, labor,
previous pregnancies, desires for boy or
girl; b) A symptom checklist; and c)
Middlesex Hospital Questionnaire (to
measure somatic symptoms). 4) Transient
depressive mood swing within 10 days of
delivery ("maternity blues"). 6) 38 out
of 50 mothers (or 76%) experienced
maternity blues. Author states the
incidence of postpartum blues in this
group of East Africans is similar to that
which has been noted in other cultures.

252. Harris, J.S.
1936 "A Mental Disorder Associated with
Childbearing." BR. MED. J. 1:835-837.

253. Harris, M.J.
1976 "Pediatrics Communications with the
Post-partum Patient." MED. J. AUST.
2(11):417-420.

254. Harris, Martha.
1975 "Some Notes on Maternal Containment
in 'Good Enough' Mothering." J. CHILD
PSYCHOTHERAPY 4(1):35-51.

255. Harris, R.J., and M.W. Linn.
1979 "The Need to Be Held: State or Trait
Variable." J. CLIN. PSYCHIAT.
40(6):253-257.

256. Harrison, M.J., and S.A. Hicks.
1983 "Postpartum Concerns of Mothers and
Their Sources of Help." CAN. J. PUBL.
HEALTH 74(5):325-328.

257. Hart, Donn V.
1965 SOUTHEAST ASIAN BIRTH CUSTOMS: THREE
STUDIES IN HUMAN REPRODUCTION. New
Haven, Conn.: Human Relations Area
Files.

258. Hatrick, J.A.
1976 "Puerperal Mental Illness." NURS.
TIMES 72(14): 553-554.

259. Haworth, N.A., and M.A. Camb.
1939 "Malnutrition and Debility in
Puerperal Psychosis." LANCET 2:417-418.

260. Hayworth, J.; B.C. Little; S. Bonham
Carter; P. Raptopoulos; R.G. Priest; and
M. Sandler.
1980 "A Predictive Study of Postpartum
Depression--Some Predisposing
Characteristics." BR. J. MED. PSYCHOL.
53:161-167.

1) Prospective study. 2) 166 women
attending a prenatal clinic in London. 3)
Women were assessed at 36 weeks of
pregnancy using the Hostility and
Direction of Hostility Questionnaire,
Rotter's Locus of Control Scale, and the
Delusions-Symptoms-States Inventory.
Women were mailed the Self-Rating
Depression Scale 6 weeks postpartum. 4)
Depressive illness of neurotic degree of
intensity, distinct from the shorter-lived
3-day blues, as well as from the more
florid depressive psychosis. 5)
Self-Rating Depression Scale. 6) High

anxiety and high hostility before birth
were positively associated with postnatal
depression. Women who perceived
themselves as less in control of their
lives were likely to rate high on
depression postnatally.

261. Hazle, Nancy R.
1982 "Postpartum Blues: Assessment and
Intervention." J. NURSE-MIDWIFERY
27(6):21-25.

1) Summary. 4) Subjective description of
symptoms including: tearfulness,
despondency, poor concentration,
forgetfulness, anxiety, irritation,
restlessness, disturbance in thought
processes, and inability to cope with the
infant. 7) Author recommends Crisis
Intervention where the health care
professional helps the new mother to gain
correct cognitive perception of situation;
manage affect through awareness and
verbalization of feelings; and develop
patterns of adequate support
interpersonally or within community.

262. Hazle, N.R.
1982 "Postpartum Blues--Assessment and
Intervention." J. NURSE-MIDWIFERY
27(6):21-25.

263. Hegarty, A.B.
1955 "Post-puerperal Recurrent
Depression." BR. MED. J. 1:637-640.

264. Heitler, S., and K. McCrensky.
1976 "Postpartum Depression: A
Multi-Dimensional Study." DISS. ABSTR.
INTL. 36(11-B):5792-5793.

265. Hemphill, R.E.
1952 "Incidence and Nature of Puerperal
Psychiatric Illness." BR. MED. J.
2:1232-1235.

266. Herrenkohl, Ellen C., and Roy C.
Herrenkohl.
1979 "A Comparison of Abused Children and
Their Nonabused Siblings." J. AM. ACAD.
CHILD PSYCHIAT. 18(2):260-269.

267. Herskovits, Melville J.
1937 LIFE IN A HAITIAN VALLEY. New York:
Alfred A. Knopf.

1) Ethnographic. 2) Mirebalais culture.
6) "Before mating of any type is
consummated, the familial spirits must be
notified of the approaching event so that
they may be well disposed toward it, for
no union where this is neglected can enjoy
happiness or peace. One Mirebalais woman
was pointed out as an object lesson of the
necessity of doing this. Though a devotee
of several gods, neither she nor her
husband was willing to perform the
necessary rites for her gods before their
marriage. She was suffering from an acute
case of melancholia after the birth of her
first child, and the prevailing opinion
was that she was going mad because of the
neglect of her duty toward her deities"
(p. 110).

268. Herzog, A., et al.
1976 "Psychotic Reactions Associated with
Childbirth." DISEASE OF THE NERVOUS
SYSTEM 37(4): 229-235.

60

269. Hobbs, D.F.
1965 "Parenthood as Crisis: A Third
Study." J. MARR. FAM. 27:367-372.

270. Hoch, A., and G. Kirby.
1919 "A Clinical Study of Psychoses
Characterized by Distressed Perplexity."
ARCH. NEUROL. & PSYCHIAT. 1:415-458.

271. Hollenbeck, A.R., et al.
1984 "Labor and Delivery Medication
Influences Parent--Infant Interaction in
the First Postpartum Month." INFANT BEH.
7(2):201-209.

272. Honda, H.
1974 "Mental Disturbances of the
Postpartum Period." JAP. J. CLIN.
PSYCHIAT. 3:187-202.

273. Hopkins, J.; M. Marcus; and S.B. Campbell.
1984 "Postpartum Depression--A Critical
Review." PSYCHOL. B. 95(3):498-515.

1) Summary. 4) A disorder that is
comparable to a major or minor depressive
episode as defined by Research Diagnostic
Criteria (Spitzer, Endicott, and Robins,
1978). 6) More recent and
methodologically sound research suggests
that as many as 20% of postpartum women
may develop a mild to moderate depressive
disorder. Therefore postpartum depression
seems to have great clinical relevance and
potential for future research. 7) Authors
recommend three major areas for future
research and suggest meaningful and
valuble methods: a) Incidence; b)
Symptomatology (cites necessity for
qualitative information as normal
postpartum adjustment to clearly

distinguish normal from abnormal
reactions. Further research is needed to
elucidate symptomatology, course, and
duration of postpartum depression, and to
determine how it differs from normal
postpartum adjustment and from
nonpostpartum depression); and c) A
clarification of the relative contribution
of biological, psychological, and
social-psychological variables to this
disorder.

274. Hopwood, B.S.
1927 "Child Murder and Insanity." J. MENT.
SCI. 73:95-108.

275. Horrocks, P.
1903 "Puerperal Insanity." BR. MED. J.
1:199-201.

276. Hott, J.R.
1981 "Best Laid Plans Pre- and Postpartum
Comparison of Self and Spouse Concepts
in Primiparous Lamaze Couples Who Share
Delivery and Those Who Do Not." BIRTH
DEFECT 17(6):153-180.

277. Huffman, S., et al.
1978 "Postpartum Amenorrhea: How It Is
Affected by Maternal Nutritional
Status." SCIENCE 200:1155-1157.

278. Hughes, C.H.
1882 "Hyosciamine in Insanity Following
the Puerperal State; A Clinical Brief of
Two Cases." ST. LOUIS M. & S. J.
43:362-365.

279. Huhn, A., and K. Drenk.
     1973 "Einardnung und prognose der dor
     wochenbett-psychosen." FORTSCHR.
     NEUROL. PSYCHIAT. 7:363-377.

     1) Study appears to be retrospective. 2)
     Psychosis occuring for the first-time
     postpartum in 208 cases attending
     Rheinisches Landestrankenhaus, Bonn. 5)
     Authors are only concerned with psychosis.
     6) First manifestations of an endogenous
     psychosis is in the first 15 days
     postpartum (in about 75 of the sample)
     with three-fourths of the cases developing
     the psychosis after first pregnancy.

280. Hytten, F.E., and I. Leitch.
     1964 THE PHYSIOLOGY OF HUMAN PREGNANCY.
     London: Blackwell.

281. Impastato, D.J., and A.R. Gabriel.
     1957 "Electroshock Therapy During the
     Puerperium." J.A.M.A. 163:1017-1022.

282. Isaksson, A., et al.
     1980 "Rhythmic Changes in Estriol
     Excretion During Pregnancy." AM. J.
     OBSTET. GYNEC. 137:470-480.

283. Jackson, C., and H. Laymeyer.
     1981 POST-PARTUM DEPRESSION IN AFFECTIVE
     DISORDERS: PSYCHOPATHOLOGY AND
     TREATMENT. Chicago: Yearbook Medical
     Publishing.

284. Jackson, M.D.
     1943 "Psychoses of Pregnancy." BULL. ACAD.
     MED. TORONTO 16:197-202.

285. Jacobs, B.
1943 "Aetiological Factors and Reaction
Types in Psychoses Following
Child-Birth." J. MENT. SCI. 89:242-256.

286. Jacobides, G.M.
1957 "Adrenocorticcal Function in
Puerperal Psychoses." THESIS,
UNIVERSITY OF ATHENS, GREECE.

287. Jacobson, L.; Lennart Kaij; and Ake
Nilsson.
1965 "Postpartum Mental Disorders in an
Unselected Sample: Frequency of
Symptoms and Predisposing Factors." BR.
MED. J. 1:1640-1643.

288. Jaffee, R.
1951 "Gestation Psychosis." HAREFUAH
40-81-82.

289. James, G.W.B.
1935 "Prognosis of Puerperal Insanity."
LANCET 1:1515-1516.

290. Janik, A., and O. Chomkovicova.
1955 "Psychozy v gravidite, puerperiu a
laktaciu." BRATISL. LEK. LISTY
35:25-35.

291. Janis, Deborah L.
1977 "Postpartum Adjustment as a Function
of Husband-Related Variables." DISS.
ABSTR. INTL. 38(1-b):364.

292. Janowsky, David S.; William E. Fann; and
John M. Davis.
1971 "Monoamines and Ovarian
Hormone-Linked Sexual and Emotional
Changes: A Review." ARCH. SEXUAL BEH.
1(3):205-218.

293. Jansson, Bengt.
1963 "Psychic Insufficiencies Associated
with Childbearing." ACTA PSYCHIAT.
SCAND., 63, SUPPL. 172.

294. Jarrahi-Zadeh, A.; Francis J. Kane; R.L.
Van de Castlf; P.A. Lachenbruch; and
J.A. Ewing.
1969 "Emotional and Cognitive Changes in
Pregnancy and the Early Puerperium."
BR. J. PSYCHIAT. 115:797-805.

295. Jelly, A.C.
1901 "Puerperal Insanity." BOSTON MED. &
SURG. J. 144(12):271-275.

296. Jimenez, Marcia Houdek.
1978 "Relationships Between Job
Orientation in Women and Adjustment to
the First Pregnancy and Postpartum
Period." DISS. ABSTR. INTL.
38(8-B):3886.

297. John, Jacob; Charles S.X. Seethalakshmi;
and Abraham Verghese.
1977 "Psychiatric Disturbance During the
Postpartum Period: A Prospective Study."
INDIAN J. PSYCHIAT. 19(4):40-43. (POONA)

298. Johnson, Suzanne Hall.
1979 HIGH-RISK PARENTING: NURSING
ASSESSMENT AND STRATEGIES FOR THE FAMILY
AT RISK. Philadelphia: J.B. Lippincott
Co.

299. Johnstone, R.W., and R.J. Kellar.
     1968 A TEXTBOOK OF MIDWIFERY FOR STUDENTS
     AND PRACTITIONERS. 21st EDITION.
     (Originally published 1913.) London:
     Adam and Charles Black.

     1) Summary. 6) From the obstetric point
     of view the frequency of puerperal
     insanity is about one case in 800-1000
     confinements. Heredity and personal
     predispositions play a part in its
     etiology. Primiparae and "elderly"
     primiparae are more susceptible to the
     illness. Insanity usually occurs in the
     first week postpartum and the most
     significant warning symptom is persistent
     insomnia. Recovery follows after a few
     months in about 80% of cases and
     improvement is usually associated with
     return of menstruation. "Lactational
     insanity" is a more depressed and
     melancholic type. It is more common after
     the fourth month and under treatment there
     is a 70% recovery rate. 7) various types
     of treatment are offered for each symptom
     and "... in all but the mildest cases the
     patient should be sent to a mental
     hospital."

300. Jolly, Ph.
     1911 "Beitrag zur statistk and klinik der
     puerperalpsychosen." ARCH. PSYCHIAT.
     48:792-823.

301. Jones, R.
     1902 "Puerperal Insanity." BR. MED. J.
     1:579-585.

302. Jones, W.H.S.
1923 HIPPOCRATES WITH AN ENGLISH
TRANSLATION. VOLUME I. London:
Heinemann.

303. Jordan, Briggitte.
1978 BIRTH IN FOUR CULTURES: A
CROSSCULTURAL INVESTIGATION OF CHILBIRTH
IN YUCATAN, HOLLAND, SWEDEN AND THE
UNITED STATES. MONOGRAPHS IN WOMEN'S
STUDIES. Quebec, Canada: Eden Press
Women's Publications.

304. _____. 1980 BIRTH IN FOUR CULTURES: A
CROSSCULTURAL INVESTIGATION OF
CHILDBIRTH IN YUCATAN, HOLLAND, SWEDEN
AND THE UNITED STATES. MONOGRAPHS IN
WOMEN'S STUDIES. Quebec, Canada: Eden
Press Women's Publications.

305. Kadrmas, A.; G. Winokur; and R. Crowe.
1979 "Postpartum Mania." BR. J. PSYCHIAT.
135:551-554.

306. Kaij, Lennart, and Ake Nilsson.
1964 "Mental Disorders Following
Parturition." ACTA PSYCHIAT. SCAND.
(SUPPLE.) 180:189-190.

307. Kaij, Lennart; L. Jacobson; and Ake
Nilsson.
1967 "Postpartum Mental Disorder in an
Unselected Sample: The Influence of
Parity." J. PSYCHOSOM. RES.
10(4):317-325.

308. Kaines, S.H.
1941 "The Treatment of Psychiatric States
Following Pregnancy." ILLINOIS M. J.
80:200-204.

309. Kane, Frances J., and Martin H. Keller.
     1965 "The Use of Enovid in Postpartum
     Mental Disorders." SOUTHERN MED. J.
     58:1089-1092.

310. Kane, Frances J., et al.
     1966 "Oral Contraceptives as
     Psychopharmacologic Agents." CURR.
     PSYCHIAT. THERAPY 6:219-221.

311. Kane, Francis J.; R. Daly; John A. Ewing;
     and Martin H. Keller.
     1967 "Mood and Behavioral Changes with
     Progestational Agents." BR. J.
     PSYCHIAT. 113:265-268.

312. Kane, Francis J.; William J. Harman, Jr.;
     Martin H. Keller; and John A. Ewing.
     1968 "Emotional and Cognitive Disturbance
     in the Early Puerperium." BR. J.
     PSYCHIAT. 114(506):99-102.

313. Kane, Frances J., Jr.; Peter A.
     Lachenbruch; Lee Lokey; Neil Chafetz;
     Richard Auman; Leo Pocuis; and Morris A.
     Lipton.
     1971 "Postpartum Depression in Southern
     Black Women." DISEASES OF THE NERVOUS
     SYSTEM 32(7):486-489.

1) Prospective. 2) Samples of obstetrical
patients who delivered on the maternity
ward of the North Carolina Memorial
Hospital, Chapel Hill, during the summers
of 1968 and 1969 were taken. Of a group
of 126 black married females and 132
whites, only 8% of the black cohorts and
58% of the white cohorts had education
beyond high school. Greater frequency of
grand multiparity (>4 offspring) in
blacks, 38% versus 4% in whites. 3) The

patients were interviewed on the second or
third day postpartum and were administered
a semi-structured interview relating to
contraceptive use, demographic data and
information concerning menstrual history,
and each cohort also completed the
Neuroticism Scale Questionnaire. 4) The
postpartum period was defined as the
second or third day for purposes of this
study. 5) Neuroticism Scale
Questionnaire. 6) Black patients tended
to cluster themselves at the extremes of
personality traits (e.g., more kindly, or
helpless, or practical and responsible,
more often cheerful and extroverted, etc.)
The blacks reported significantly less
anxiety (p < 0.08) and higher neuroticism
scores, 27% versus 18% in white patients.
The whites showed a significant increase
in self-rating of depression.

314. Kaplan, E.H., and L.H. Blackman.
     1969 "The Husband's Role in Psychiatric
     Illness Associated with Childbearing."
     PSYCHIAT. QUART. 43(3):396-409.

315. Karacan, I., et al.
     1969 "Some Implications of the Sleep
     Patterns of Pregnancy for Postpartum
     Emotional Disturbances." BR. J.
     PSYCHIAT. 115:929-935.

316. Karnosh, L.J., and J.M. Hope.
     1937 "Puerperal Psychoses and Their
     Sequellae." AM. J. PSYCHIAT.
     94:537-550.

317. Kato, Yuichi.
     1974 "Psychopathological Investigation of
     Postpartum Depression." JAP. J. CLIN.
     PSYCHIAT. 3(4):373-379.

318. Katona-Apte, J.
     1973 "The Relevance of Nourishment tc the
          Reproductive Cycle of the Female in
          India." In: BEING FEMALE. (Dana
          Raphael,ed.)

319. Kear-Colwell, J.J.
     1965 "Neuroticism in the Early
          Puerperium." BR. J. PSYCHIAT.
          111:1189-1192.

320. Kelly, J.V.
     1967 "The Influence of Native Customs on
          Obstetrics in Nigeria." OBSTETRICS AND
          GYNECOLOGY 30:608-612.

     1) Commentary. 2) Two years' observation
     as staff obstetrician in Nigerian Tribal
     Hospital. 6) Brief description of birth
     customs and role of traditional medicine
     amoung Ibibio tribe. While critical of
     traditional practices author finds
     postpartum depression rare. Suggests that
     social structure and postpartum rituals
     play a role in prevention, especially the
     2-3 month seclusion in "fattening room."

321. Keller, Martin H.; Francis J. Kane; and R.
        Daly.
     1964 "An Acute Schizophrenic Episode
          Following Abrupt Withdrawal of Enovid in
          a Patient with Previous Post-partum
          Psychiatric Disorder." AM. J. PSYCHIAT.
          120:1123-1124.

322. Kendell, R.E.
     1978 "Childbirth as an Aetiological
          Agent." In: MENTAL ILLNESS IN PREGNANCY
          AND THE PUERPERIUM. London: Oxford. pp.
          69-79.

     1) Retrospective. 2) 2257 mothers and
     2116 fathers were obtained from a city
     register of still and live births. 3)
     They werre studied retrospectively 2 years
     prior to the birth of the child and
     followed through for 2 years after. 4) "A
     sharp rise in the incidence of functional
     psychosis." 5) The total numbers of
     mothers and fathers under psychiatric care
     were tabulated for the four years of the
     study. 6) There was a clear-cut rise in
     the new episode rate after delivery for
     all diagnostic criteria, including the
     "blues," depression, and functional
     psychoses. In the fathers the event
     produced no rise in the new episode rate,
     suggesting that "father" depression is not
     widespread. Events that might be expected
     to be stressful--stillbirth, twins, and
     illegitimate births--all failed to
     increase the risk of puerperal illness.

323. Kendell, R.E.; S. Wainwright; A. Hailey;
     and B. Shannon.
     1976 "The Influence of Childbirth on
          Psychiatric Mortality." PSYCHOL. MED.
          6(2):297-302.

324. Kendell, R.E.; D. Rennie; J.A. Clarke; and
     C. Dean.
     1981 "The Social and Obstetric Correlates
          of Psychiatric Admission in the
          Puerperium." PSYCHOL. MED. 11:341-350.

325. Ketai, Richard M., and Marvin A. Bradwin.
     1979 "Childbirth-Related Psychosis and
     Familial Symbiotic Conflict." AM. J.
     PSYCHIAT. 136:190-193.

326. Kilpatrick, E., and H.M. Tiebout.
     1926 "A Study of Psychoses Occurring in
     Relationship to Childbirth." AM. J.
     PSYCHIAT. 6:145-159.

327. Kitlin, V.P., et al.
     1975 "Classification and Clinical Course
     of Puerperal Psychoses." VRACH DELO
     12:99-101 (ENG. ABSTRACT).

328. Kitzinger, Sheila.
     1975 "The Fourth Trimester." MIDWIFE
     HEALTH VISITOR 11(4): 118-121.

329. _____.
     1980 WOMEN AS MOTHERS: HOW THEY SEE
     THEMSELVES IN DIFFERENT CULTURES. New
     York: Vintage Books.

330. Klaus, M.; R. Jer Auld; N. Kreger; W.
     McAlpine; M. Steffa; and J. Kennell.
     1972 "Maternal Attachment: Importance of
     the First Post-partum Days." NEW ENGL.
     J. MED. 286:460-463.

331. Klaus, M.A., and J.H. Kennell.
     1976 MATERNAL-INFANT BONDING. St. Louis:
     C.V. Mosby Co. p.1-15

332. Klein, F.; N. Marchand; and C. Klein.
1979 "Psychopathology of the Small Child:
Attempt at Preventing Early Childhood
Disturbances by Means of Preliminary
Research on a Longitudinal Study of
Pregnant Women and Their Children."
NEUROPSYCHIATRIE DE L'ENFANCE ET DE
L'ADOLESCENCE 27(12):495-504.

1) Prospective. 2) Case histories and
longitudinal interviews of
psychopathological disorders in young
children (less than 6 years) attending the
school of infant neuropsychology in paris,
were conducted. 6) Authors attempt to
determine the psychogenic origin of
psychosis in the young child. A
relationship among child psychosis and
postpartum depression and "mourning" is
explored.

333. Kleinberg, Warren M.
1977 "Counseling Mothers in the Hospital
Postpartum Period: A Comparison of
Techniques." AM. J. PUBLIC HEALTH
67(7):672-674.

334. Kline, C.L.
1955 "Emotional Illness Associated with
Childbirth." AM. J. OBSTET. GYNEC.
69:748-757.

335. Knapp, Robert C., and David H. Drucker.
1972 "Self-Inflicted Stab Wounds to
Pregnant Uterus and Fetus at Term." NEW
YORK STATE J. MED. 72(3):391-392.

336. Korkina, M.V.; M.Y. Tsivilko; M.A. Karera;
     and A.V. Dougy.
     1983 "Catatono-Onerroidal Paroxysms of
     Schizophrenia Manifested in the
     Postpartum Period." ZH NEUR PS
     83(11):1702-1707. (RUSSIAN)

337. Kraepelin, I.
     1913 LECTURES ON CLINICAL PSYCHIATRY. 3rd
     ENGLISH EDITION. London: Baillieve,
     Tindall and Cassel.

338. Kruckman, Laurence, and Chris
     Asmann-Finch.
     In Press. "Postpartum 'Blues' in
     Appalachia and Southern Illinois."
     CULTURE, ILLNESS AND PSYCHIATRY.

1) Point study. 2) 30 new mothers from S.
Appalachia and 58 woman from rural
southern Illinois were selected from
birthing centers. 3) An adapted Zung
Depression Scale and a 54-item
questionnaire were used to measure
depression and levels of support, and
satisfaction with current status. Further,
an open ended interview recored
information regarding emotional and
task-oriented support. 4) Depression
determined by Zung scores. 5) Zung
Depression Scale. 6) The lack of
emotional and task-oriented support is
strongly correlated with a negative
postpartum experience. However, the
authors challenge the assumption that
quantity of support is an important
predictive tool; quality spousal support,
both task and emotional oriented is a
critical factor. In addition, social
support and recognition of role change may
determine the type of birth experience a

woman has.

339. Kruckman, Lawrence; June Craig; and Sharon
     Svennson.
     1980 "A Little Victory Everyday: Coping
     with Postpartum Problems." (Film, 37
     minutes.) UNIVERSITY OF WISCONSIN MEDIA
     SERVICES, Kenosha, Wisconsin.

340. Kukull, Walter A., and Donald R. Peterson.
     1977 "Sudden Infant Death and
     Infanticide." AM. J. EPID.
     106(6):485-486.

341. Kumar, R., and Kay Robson.
     1978 "Neurotic Disturbance During
     Pregnancy and the Puerperium:
     Prelimiary Report of a Prospective
     Survey of 119 Primiparae." In: MENTAL
     ILLNESS IN PREGNANCY AND THE PUERPERIUM.
     (Merton Sandler, ed.) Oxford: Oxford
     University Press.

     1) Prospective--retrospective. 2) 114
     primiparae, average age, 28. 3) All were
     interviewed by a psychologist at 12 weeks,
     the 24th weeks, and the 36th week of
     pregnancy. They were interviewed by a
     psychiatrist at about the 13th or 14th
     week of pregnancy and about 3 months after
     the birth of their babies. 6) The
     retrospective view of three months before
     pregnancy as compared to the 1st trimester
     shows a sharp increase in the incidence of
     depression. Marital tensions during
     pregnancy, original doubts about going
     through with the pregnancy, difficult
     relations with their own parents, age over
     30 years and, trying to conceive for two
     or more years, were all more likely to be
     factors causing depression. There was no

link between antenatal and postnatal
depression and this may suggest rather
different patterns of vulnerability at
these times.

342. _____.
1978 "Previous Induced Abortion and
Ante-natal Depression in Primiparae:
Prelimiary Report of a Survey of Mental
Health in Pregnancy." PSYCHOL. MED.
8:711-715.

343. Kumar, R., et al.
1981 "Childbearing and Maternal Sexuality:
A Prospective Survey of 119 Primiparae."
J. PSYCHOSOM. RES. 25:373-83.

344. Kumar, R.; S. Isaacs; and E. Meltzerr.
1983 "Recurrent Postpartum Psychosis--A
Model for Prospective Clinical
Investigation." BR. J. PSYCHIAT.
142(Jun):618-620.

345. Laderman, Carol.
1983 WIVES & MIDWIVES: CHILDBIRTH &
NUTRITIAN IN RURAL MALAYSIA. Berkeley:
University of California Pres.

1) Ethnography with prospective study
concerning diet. 2) 140 women, source of
informantS unclear. 3) In-depth
interviews & observation. 6) Chapter 7
focuses on the postpartum period and
represents one of the most complete
ethnographic descriptions of rituals
related to childbirth. The pantang, a
35-36 day series of rituals, dictary
constraints, is fully outlined. It is
stressed that the rituals are for the
mother's, not her baby's, sake. 98% still
use the salaian or "roosting bed" thought

to reduce ritual impurity, increase blood
circulation, and close up the cervix. By
collecting blood samples (N=8) and
analyzing diet, the author concludes that
the study group's dietary restrictions did
not play a role in anemia or thiamine
deficiency.

346. Ladisich, W.
     1974 "Effect of Progesterone on Regional
     5-Hydroxytryptamine Metabolism in the
     Rat Brain." NEUROPHARMACOLOGY
     13(9):877-883.

347. Langdon, F.W.
     1915 "Insanities of the Puerperal State."
     LANCET 1:296-300.

348. Larsen, Virginia L.; Theodora Evans; and
     Loretta Martin.
     1967 "Differences Between New Mothers:
     Psychiatric Admissions Versus Normals."
     J. AM. MED. WOMEN'S ASSOC. 22:955-958.

349. Leiderman, P.H., et al.
     1975 "Mother-Infant Neonatal Separation:
     Some Delayed Consequences." CIBA.
     FOUND. SYMP. 33:213-239.

350. Leifer, Myra.
     1980 PSYCHOLOGICAL EFFECTS OF MOTHERHOOD,
     A STUDY OF FIRST PREGNANCY. University
     of Chicago Press. 304 pp.

351. Lennane, K., and R. Lennane.
     1973 "Alleged Psychogenic Disorders in
     Women: A Possible Manifestation of
     Sexual Prejudice." NEW ENGL. J. MED.
     288(6):288-292.

352. Leonard, L.G.
     1981 "Postpartum Depression and Mothers of
          Infant Twins." MATERN. CHILD NURS. J.
          10(2):99-109.

     1) Psychiatric case study. 2) Three
     mothers of twins involved in counseling
     sessions at postpartum counseling agency
     in Vancouver, B.C. These mothers were
     seeking assistance for symptoms related to
     depression. 3) Counseling sessions at
     2.5, 4.5, and 6 months post-delivery. 4)
     Postpartum depression is linked with
     failure to perform the parental, marital,
     and individual roles in a satisfying
     manner. 6) Author believes nursing has a
     responsibility to try to prevent emotional
     difficulties in the postpartum period, to
     recognize postpartum depression, and to
     more effectively support parents during
     the depressive crisis. 7) Nursing
     interventions are highly recommended for
     mothers of twins. They include: a)
     Assessment of parents' ability to cope in
     early postpartum period; b) Assistance in
     conflict resolution and problem-solving;
     helping parents obtain desired family and
     community supports; c) Encouragement for
     both parents to seek counseling if needed;
     d) Pre-natal education and guidance if
     parents are expecting twins.

353. Lesh, A.
     1978 "Postpartum Depression." CURR. PRACT.
          OBSTET. GYNEC. NURS. 2:52-64.

354. Levenson, D.; C. Darrow; E. Klein; M.
          Levenson; and B. McKee.
     1978 THE SEASONS OF A WOMAN'S LIFE. New
          York: Knopf.

355. Levine, R.A.
     1963 "Child Rearing in Sub-Saharan Africa:
     An Interim Report." BULL. MENN. CLIN.
     27(5):245-246.

356. Lewis, D.O.
     1974 "The Pharmacodynamics of Depression
     and Its Relation to Therapy." BR. J.
     CLIN. PRAC. 28(1):21-27.

357. Lewis, P.J.; W. Ironside; P. McKinnon; and
     C.W. Simons.
     1974 "The Karitane Project: Psychological
     Ill-Health, Infant Distress and the
     Postpartum Period." NZ. MED. J.
     79(517):1005-1009.

358. Lieberman, J.
     1954 "Postpartum Psychosess--A Review." M.
     BULL. UNIV. SOUTHERN CAL. 6:9-14.

359. Lindsay, J.S.
     1975 "Puerperal Psychosis: A Follow-Up
     Study of a Joint Mother and Baby
     Treatment Program." AUST. NZ. J.
     PSYCHIAT. 9(2):73-76.

360. Linn, L.
     1941 "The Psychoses of Pregnancy." DIS.
     NERV. SYSTEM 2:290-295.

361. Lipkin, Gladys B.
     1971 "Antepartal Anticipatory Guidance
     Conferences and Postpartum Blues."
     Masters Thesis, Adelphi University,
     Garden City, New York.

362. Little, B.C.; J. Hayworth; P. Benson; L.R.
     Bridge; J. Dewhurst; and R.G. Priest.
     1982 "Psychophysiological Antenatal
     Prediction of Postnatal Depressed Mood."
     J. PSYCHOSOM. 26(4):419-428.

363. Livingood, Amy Bookman.
     1977 "The Depressed Mother as a Source of
     Stimulation for Her Infant."   DISS.
     ABSTR. INT. 37(11-B):5835.

364. Livingston, J.E.; P.M. MacLeod; and D.A.
     Applegarth.
     1978 "Vitamin B6 Status in Women with
     Postpartum Depression."   AM. J. CLIN.
     NUTR. 31(5):886-891.

1) Point study.   2) The subjects were 40
nonpregnant women of reproductive age
(control), 30 pregnant women, 20
postpartum but not depressed (postpartum
control), and 24 postpartum depressed
women.   3) Vitamin B6 levels were obtained
using EGOT Test.   The depression level was
determined by the Beck Depression
Inventory Score and the Depression
Adjective Check List.   The postpartum, not
depressed, were tested between 1 and 6.5
months postpartum.   The postpartum,
depressed, were tested between 2 weeks and
4 years postpartum.   The pregnant women
were tested between the 11th and 39th
weeks of pregnancy.   5) The Beck
Depression Inventory and the Depression
Adjective Checklist.   6) The mean of the
EGOT for the group of postpartum depressed
patients did not differ significantly from
the mean of the nonpregnant control group,
the pregnant group, or the postpartum, not
depressed.   The mean EGOT for the
postpartum depressed patients was

significantly higher for the four patients
that were taking large B6 supplements.
The mean Depression Scores, particularly
the Beck, were lower in the postpartum
depressed patients taking B6 supplements
than in those not taking B6, but the
differences were not significant. There
was found to be no evidence of vitamin B6
deficiency in women suffering with
postpartum depression.

365. Lloyd, J.H.
      1889 A SYSTEM OF OBSTETRICS. VOLUME II.
         Philadelphia: Len Brothers.

366. Lloyd, Barbara B.
      1970 "Yoruba Mothers' Reports of
         Child-Rearing: Some Theoretical and
         Methodological Considerations." In:
         SOCIALIZATION. (P. Mayer, ed.) New
         York: Travistock.

367. Lomas, P.
      1960 "The Husband-Wife Relationship in
         Cases of Puerperal Breakdown." BR. J.
         MED. PSYCHOL. 32:117-123.

368. _____.
      1960 "Defensive Organization and Puerperal
         Breakdown." BR. J. MED. PSYCHOL.
         33:61-66.

369. Loo, P.; S. Saba; J. Sauvage; H. Loo; and
         Y. Pouzols.
      1971 "Une Demence Puerperale?" SOCIETE
         MEDICO-PSYCHOLOGIQUE 129(2):592-600.

370. Lowenstein, Herzl.
      1969 "Mental Disorder and Childbirth."
         LANCET 7600:887.

371. Ludington-Hoe, S.M.
     1977 "POSTPARTUM: DEVELOPMENT OF
     MATERNITY." AM. J. NURS.
     77(7):1171-1174.

372. Luepker, Ellen T.
     1972 "Joint Admission and Evaluation of
     Postpartum Psychiatric Patients and
     Their Infants." HOSPITAL COMMUNITY
     PSYCHIATRY 23(9):284-287.

373. Luft, Arbeit Von Helmut.
     1964 "Die Wochenbettdepression. Klinik and
     Pathogenetische Faktoren." DER
     NERVENARZT 35(5):185-194.

374. Lukianowicz, N.
     1971 "Infanticide." PSYCHIAT. CLIN.
     4:145-158.

375. Lyter, Sharon C., and Lloyd L. Lyter.
     1979 "Encountering Personal Crisis: A
     Subjective Account of Caesarean
     Childbirth." VOICES 15(1):71-75.

376. MacCormack, Carol P.
     1982 ETHNOGRAPHY OF FERTILITY AND BIRTH.
     New York: Academic Press.

377. MacCormack, M.J.
     1839 "Cases of Puerperal Mania with a
     Dissection and Remarks." LANCET
     1:549-551.

378. MacDonald, Carlos F.
     1899 "Puerperal Insanity. A Cursory View
     for the General Practitioner." MEDICAL
     RECORD 55(7).

379. MacDonald, J.
     1847 "Puerperal Insanity." AM. J. INSAN.
     4:113-163.

380. MacKenzie, Shirley J.
     1977 "A Mother Care Class." TRANSACTIONAL
     ANAL. 7(1):68-70.

381. MacLeod, M.D.
     1886 "An Address on Puerperal Insanity."
     BR. MED. J. 2:239-242.

382. Main, T.F.
     1958 "Mothers with Children in a
     Psychiatric Hospital." LANCET
     7:845-847.

383. Malleson, J.
     1953 "An Endocrine Factor in Certain
     Affective Disorders." LANCET 2:158-164.

384. _____.
     1963 "Association with Postpartum Mental
     Illness and Premenstrual Tension." BR.
     MED. J. 2:158.

385. Malnory, Margaret E.
     1982 "A Prenatal Assessment Tool for
     Mothers and Fathers." J.
     NURSE-MIDWIFERY 27(6):26-34.

     1) Summary. 3) Interview-observation
     assessment tool administered 4 times: a)
     First prenatal visit; b) The second
     trimester; c) The early third trimester;
     and d) At term. Interview-observation
     includes developmental tasks, expected
     behaviors, and nursing interventions. 4)
     Insufficient achievement of developmental
     tasks of pregnancy and childbirth.
     (Postpartum period is only alluded to in
     terms of anticipation, plans.) 5)
     Developmental tasks such as "binding-in"
     to role change, "giving of oneself,"
     realistic expectations of postpartum. 7)

Assessment and intervention
(education/guidance) comprise the
treatment plan.

386. Manton, W.P.
1892 "Puerperal Hysteria (Insanity ?)." J.
AM. MED. ASSOC. 19:61-62.

387. Marce, L.V.
1858 TRAITE DE LA FOLIE DES FEMMES
ENCEINTES, DES NOUVELLES ACCOUCHEES ET
DES NOURRICES. Paris: J.B. Bailliere.

388. Markham, S.
1961 "A Comparative Evaluation of
Psychotic and Non-psychotic Reactions to
Childbirth." AMER. J. ORTHOPSYCHIAT.
31:565-578.

389. Martin, M.E.
1958 "Puerperal Mental Illness: A
Follow-Up Study of 75 Cases." BR. MED.
J. 2:773-777.

390. _____.
1977 "A Maternity Hospital Study of
Psychiatric Illness Associated with
Childbirth." IRISH J. MED. SCI.
146:239-244.

391. Mayberger, H.W., and H.A. Abramson.
1980 "The Psychodynamics of Transitory
Postpartum Depressive Reactions." J.
ASTHMA RESEARCH 17(2):59-64.

392. McDermaid, G., and E.G. Winkler.
1955 "Psychopathology of Infanticide." J.
CLIN. EXPER. PSYCHOPATH. 16:22-41.

393. McGeorge, J.
1938 "Mental Disorder and Childbirth."
MED. J. AUST. 2(17):671-677.

394. McGoogan, L.S.
1933 "The Toxic Psychoses of Pregnancy and
the Puerperium." AM. J. OBSTET. GYNEC.
25:792-799.

395. McGowan, M.N.
1977 "Postpartum Disturbance: A Review of
the Literature in Terms of Stress
Response." J. NURSE MIDWIFE 22(2):27-34.

396. McIlroy, A. Louise.
1927 "Nervous and Mental Health of the
Mother During Pregnancy, Labor and the
Puerperium." MATERNITY & CHILD WELFARE
11:349-352.

397. _____.
1928 "The Influence of Parturition Upon
Insanity and Crime." BR. MED. J.
72:303-304.

398. McKenzie, C.A.; M.E. Canaday; and E.
Carroll.
1982 "Comprehensive care during the
postpartum period." NURS. CLIN. NORTH
AM. 17:23-48.

399. McKinlay, J.B.
1972 "The Sick Role: Illness and
Pregnancy." SOC. SCI. MED.
6(5):561-572.

1) Theoretical. 6) It is argued that,
although women who are pregnant occupy a
special position in society and in certain
situations fulfill unique expectations,
this normal state cannot be considered a

form of illness according to Parson's sick role paradigm. However, it is argued that this relatively unstructured situation in the U.S. during most of the period of gestation (and childbirth) is likely to produce a sense of role ambiguity or strain on women.

400. McNair, F.E.
1952 "Psychosis Occurring Postpartum: Analysis of 34 Cases." CANAD. MED. ASSOC. J. 67:637-641.

1) Retrospective. 2) Thirty-six patients were found from all cases of psychosis occuring postpartum admitted to the Crease Clinic of Psychological Medicine, Essondale, British Columbia between 1 March 1944 and 30 September 1951. For inclusion in the study patients met the following criteria: a) First attack of mental illness directly following childbirth; b) Prenatal psychotic symptoms absent even in retrospect; c) Admission to psychiatric hospital ward within one day after parturition; and d) Toxemia of pregnancy not apparent or minimal. 4) A definition of the postpartum period developed after review of all cases meeting above criteria. The eventual definition of the postpartum period was birth to one year. 5) Author mentions that 34 of the patients would classify as having a schizo-affective psychosis as classified by the international nomenclature. His further comments seem to indicate that he accepted schizo-affective, catatonic schizophrenis, and puerperal psychosis/anxiety as labelled by the attending physician and not by a standard before mentioned

combination of symptoms. 6) There appeared to be a sequential relationship between delivery and the onset of psychosis. Similarities between cases included: a) Onset of illness was acute and dramatic within 10 days following delivery; b) No patient was under 21 or over 39, 24 out of 34 were 25 or older at the time of the first attack; c) 19 out of the 32 were primiparae; d) 21 out of 32 bore girls; e) 15 out of 32 were the youngest daughters in their family; f) Family psychopathology was present in 12 out of 36 cases; and, g) only 3 patients spent less than 3 months in the institution. (Size of each sample varies due to restrictions of inclusion for each criterion. Tests of statistical significance were not conducted.) Salient features of symptomology were those characteristic of schizophrenia (e.g., hallucinations, aggression, hostility, etc.)

401. Mead, Margaret, and Niles Newton.
1967 "Cultural Patterning of Perinatal Behavior." In: CHILDBEARING: ITS SOCIAL AND PSYCHOLOGICAL ASPECTS. (S.A. Richardson and A.F. Guttmacher, eds.) Baltimore: Williams and Wilkins.

402. Meares, Russel; James Grimwade; and Carl Wood.
1976 "A Possible Relationship Between Anxiety in Pregnancy and Puerperal Depression." J. PSYCHOSOM. RES. 20(6):605-610.

1) Prospective. 2) The sample population was defined as all married women attending the Antenatal Clinic at Queens Victoria

Hospital; one hundred and twenty-nine
women participated in the study. Those
patients whose native language was not
english were excluded. 3) Interviews were
conducted on the first antenatal visit at
a standard time on a particular day in
consecutive weeks. A second portion of
the study included mailed-in
questionnaires after the original set of
interviews were completed. (Only 49 of
the original 129 replied.) 4) Birth to five
months, inclusive, was defined as the
postpartum period for the first half of
the study; six to eighteen months,
inclusive, was defined as the second half.
5) The Taylor Manifest Anxiety Scale was
used to determine levels of anxiety and
the Eysenck Personality Inventory was used
to determine levels of neuroticism.
Visual Analogy Scales were administered.
Additionally, women were asked to scale
the following questions: a) I felt
miserable and depressed; b) I had spells
of crying; c) I felt without hope; d) I
felt useless and a burden to others. If
present after completing the scale, women
were asked the length of their depression
and if they had sought treatment. Those
patients whose experience of misery and
depression was greater than one-half the
time and felt a burden more than one-half
the time that persisted more than a month
were judged to be depressed. If a woman
received treatment for depression, she was
also judged to be depressed. 6) The range
of incidence of postpartum depression was
10-16. Four kinds of puerperal mood
change were distinguished using the visual
analogy scales. Puerperal depression can
be predicted by the levels of anxiety
experienced during pregnancy.

403. MEDICAL WORLD NEWS, Editors of.
     1976 "Postpartum Blues: A Special Entity?"
     17(14):29.

404. Megler, M., et al.
     1974 "Nurse-Midwives Make a Difference."
     NURS. OUTLOOK 22(6):386-389.

405. Melchior, L.
     1975 "Is the Postpartum Period a Time of
     Crisis For Some Mothers." CANAD. NURSE
     71(7):30-32.

406. Melges, F.T.
     1968 "Postpartum Psychiatric Syndromes."
     PSYCHOSOM. MED. 30:95-108.

407. _____.
     1969 "Postpartum Psychiatric Reactions:
     Time of Onset and Sex Ratio of
     Newborns." SCIENCE 166:1026-1027.

408. Menninger, William C.
     1943 "The Emotional Factors of Pregnancy."
     BULL. MENN. CLIN. 7:15-24.

409. Mentzos, S.
     1968 "Patogenetische und Nosologische
     Aspekte der Wochenbettpsychosen." In:
     PSYCHIATRIE UND NEUROLOGIE DER
     SCHWANGERSDAFT: FORUM DER PSYCHIATRIE.
     23, 110-119. Stuttgart: Enke.

410. Menzies, W.F.
     1893 "Puerperal Insanity: An Analysis of
     140 Consecutive Cases." AM. J. INSAN.
     50:147-185.

411. Mercer, R.T.
     1977 "Postpartum: Illness and
     Acquaintance-Attachment Process." AM.
     J. NURS. 77(7):1174-1178.

412. _____.
     1981 "Factors Impacting on the Maternal
     Role the First Year of Motherhood."
     BIRTH DEFEC. 17(6):233-252.

413. Mercer, R.T., and K. Hackley.
     1982 "Factors Correlating with Maternal
     Age Early Postpartum." NURS. RES.
     31(3):188.

414. Merrill, G.G.
     1957 "Prevention of Postpartum Psychosis."
     SOUTHERN MED. J. 50:1034-1037.

415. Mester, R., et al.
     1975 "Conjoint Hospitalization of Mother
     and Baby in Post-Partum Syndromes: Why
     and How." ISRAEL ANNALS PSYCHIATRY AND
     RELATED DISCIPLINES. 13(2):124-36.

1) Summary. 3) 8 cases of mother and baby
conjoint hospitalization. 4) Post-partum
Syndrome defined as "any psychiatric
disorder in which childbirth is one of the
interacting causal agents, a necessary but
not sufficient cause. It includes behavior
classifiable as schizophrenia, depression,
psychoneurous, organic (toxic) psychous,
and a transient situational disorder
regarded as within normal limits--the
post-partum blues." 5) The criterion used
for hospitalizing a mother with depression
along with her child were: a) Mothering
capacities. b) General personality
characteristics. And c) Motivation for
treatment.

416. Miguel, Angeles De, and Mercedes Valcarce.
     1978 "Problemas Psiquicos de la Lactancia
     Materna." REV. DE. PSIC. GRAL. Y APL.
     33:251-278.

417. Miller, M.F.
     1950 "Post-partum Deficits." TR. NEW ENGL.
     OBSTET. & GYNEC. SOC. 4:139-149.

418. Mims-Jimenez, S.L.
     1979 "Beating the Blues." AM. BABY
     41(17):16, 24.

419. Minturn, L., and W.W. Lambert.
     1964 MOTHERS OF SIX CULTURES, ANTECEDENTS
     OF CHILD REARING. New York: Wiley.

420. Molnar, G., and N.F. White.
     1972 "Concurrent Psychiatric Admissions: A
     Report on a Simultaneous Hospitalization
     of Family Members." CANADIAN PSYCHIAT.
     ASSOC. J. 17(6):449-454.

     1) Descriptive. 6) Author describes a
     four-year program to admit the families of
     affected individuals to help aid in
     recovery of the patient. The in-patient
     unit is part of the Clinical Network of
     McMaster University Department of
     Psychiatry and is located in St. Joseph's
     Hospital, Hamilton, Ontario. Fifty-six
     cases, 22 of which involved postpartum
     mental disorders, were observed for
     recovery rate. Among the conclusions
     reached, concurrent admission of affected
     women and their newborns aided
     significantly in their recovery and
     subsequent discharge.

421. Moloney, J.C.
     1952 "Post-partum Depression or Third-day
          Depression Following Childbirth." NEW
          ORLEANS CHILD-PARENT DIGEST 6:20-32.

422. Monellick, Ruth S.
     1981 "Postpartum Depression and Early
          Parental Relationship, Marital
          Adjustment, and Self-Concept." DISS.
          ABSTR. University of New Mexico.

     1) Prospective. 2) 129 primiparas white,
     middle-class mothers selected from
     childbirth education class. 3)
     Questionaires completed during the last
     trimester of pregnancy and eight weeks
     postpartum. 5) Schultz Life and
     Interpersonal History Scale; Pitt Mood
     Scale and Lock and Wallace's Marital
     Adjustment Test. 6) Significant
     relationship between mother's perception
     of the quality of their own parent-child
     experience and the level of postpartum
     depression they developed. One
     interpersonal varible, self-concept, was
     significant; a lower level of
     self-concept, the higher the probability
     of depression.

423. Montgomery, T.
     1969 "Case for Nurse-Midwives." AM. J.
          OBSTET. GYNEC. 105:309-313.

424. Moore, D.
     1983 "Prepared Childbirth and Marital
          Satisfaction During the Antepartum and
          Postpartum Periods." NURS. RES.
          32(2):73-9.

425. Morgenshy, Carole.
     1982 "Psychological and Attitudinal
     Reaction to Childbirth of Recently
     Parturient Women." DISS. ABSTR. Fordham
     University.

     1) Prospective. 2) 134 primiparas, white,
     middle class mothers, age 8 to 36. 3)
     Questionnaires administered during early
     postpartum. 5) Multiple Affect Adjective
     Check List; Rosenberg Self-Esteem Scale;
     and Rotter Internal-External Locus of
     Control Scale. 6) Mothers undergoing a
     cesarean delivery and who viewed this as a
     negative and disappointing process,
     experienced the highest levels of
     postpartum anxiety and depression. Those
     who experienced a non-cesarean delivery
     but with a complicated vaginal delivery
     presented less anxiety and depression than
     the cesarean sample but more than the
     sample with a normal vaginal delivery. 7)
     Recommends realistic training, through
     family centered maternal care units, to
     provide more accurate information
     regarding abnormal labor and delivery.

426. Morris, N.
     1972 PSYCHOSOMATIC MEDICINE IN OBSTETRICS
     AND GYNAECOLOGY. Basel: S. Karger. 656
     p.

427. Mosher, J. Montgomery.
     1909 "Puerperal Insanity." ARCH. F.
     GYNAKOL. 79:53.

428. _____ .
     1910 "Puerperal Insanity." ALBANY M. ANN.
     31:84-87.

429. Moss, Peter, and Ian Plewis.
1977 "Mental Distress in Mothers of
Pre-school Children in Inner London."
PSYCHOL. MED. 7:641-652.

1) Prospective. 2) All women with one or
more children under 5 years living in
three areas of inner London (1 in South
Camden and 2 in North Paddington) between
June 1974 and May 1975 were eligible.
Interviews were obtained from 350 women
with 454 children, a response rate of 66%.
Of those interviewed, 35% were immigrants
(i.e., born outside Britain or Ireland,
45% of them in the West Indies) and 22%
were not living with a man at the time of
the interview. Forty-four percent of the
women were middle-class and 56% working
class. 3) Women, interviewed in their own
homes, were asked questions about use of
and desire for pre-school services, child
behavior, and the mother's employment and
social contacts, mental and physical
health in the last 12 months. The term
"distress" was used to describe the
psychological state being assessed. An
assessment was made on a 4-point scale,
mothers rated 2 or 3 being regarded as
having, or having had, a moderate or
severe problem, while a rating of 1
indicated a mild problem. Interviews were
randomly allocated among a team of
interviewers, and later analysis showed no
significant differences in results gained
from each interviewer. 4) Postpartum was
defined as birth to five years. 5) It
must be noted at this point that authors
are not limiting their inquiry to the
understanding of postpartum distress but
to the whole array of adverse affects
encountered during the first 5 years

postpartum. Assessment of distress was made on the basis of questioning about feelings of worry, anxiety and depression, and associated symptoms, such as irritability, tension, suicidal thoughts, and functional impairment. Appendix 1 of the report (p. #650) lists the questions used. 6) Immigrant respondents were excluded from the analysis because of linguistic, cultural, and other possible differences. Forty-two non-immigrant mothers, whose husbands were present during the interview, were also excluded from analysis because researchers felt husbands may have had an inhibiting effect on their wives' responses. Both groups had significantly lower distress ratings. Seventy-two percent of non-married mothers had, or had had, a moderate or severe distress problem compared with 46% of married mothers. Among all the non-employed mothers, those rated as 'wants to work now' and over 50% were more likely to be distressed than those who said they did not want to work at present. Women who had lived in the same dwelling for more than 5 years were only half as likely to get a distress problem rating. Jointly relating 'length of time in house', 'housing index', and 'satisfaction with housing' to distress, showed that each of these had a significant effect on distress which was independent of the other two.

430. Moyer, John A.; Lorraine R. Herrenkohl; and David M. Jacobowitz.
     1977 "Effects of Stress During Pregnancy on Calecholamines in Discrete Brain Regions." BRAIN RESEARCH (AMSTERDAM) 121(2):385-393.

431. Nadelson, Carol.
1973 "Normal and 'Special' Aspects of
Pregnancy." OBSTET. GYNECOL.
41(4):611-620.

432. Nadelson, Carol, and Malkah T. Notman.
1977 EMOTIONAL ASPECTS OF THE SYMPTOMS,
FUNCTIONS, AND DISORDERS OF WOMEN IN
PSYCHIATRIC MEDICINE. New York:
Brunner/Mazel.

433. Naroll, F.; R. Naroll; and F. Howard.
1961 "Position of Women in Childbirth."
AM. J. OBSTET. GYNEC. 80:943-954.

434. Neumann, Gail L.
1978 "Beyond Pregnancy and Childbirth: The
Use of Anticipatory Guidance in
Preparing Couples for Postpartum
Stress." DISS. ABSTR. INTL.
38(11-B):5582.

435. Newnham, J.P., et al.
1984 "A Study of the Relationship Between
Circulating B-Endorphin-Like
Immunoreactivity and Postpartum
'Blues.'" CLIN. ENDOCRINOL. 20:169-177.

1) Prospective, with a summary. 2) 23
women in 36th week of gestation with
normal vaginal deliveries, no history of
mental illness; primiparous. 3) The women
were interveiwed at the 36th week of
gestation for personal factors (i.e., age,
social status, her view toward pregnancy,
etc.) and completed an institute of
personality and ability testing (IPAC)
questionnaire. Blood samples for
determination of B-endorphin levels were
taken then and at delivery, 1 hour
postpartum and 24 hours postpartum. The

day after delivery the women and the
midwife independently assessed the pain of
labor and delivery. On the third day
women were observed and scored for 5
"blues symptoms": anxiety, depression,
insomnia, loss of appetite, and
tearfulness. 6) Levels of B-endorphin
have been known to increase in labor and
reach a maximum at delivery but not as
great as was found in this study. A
negative correlation was found between the
woman's estimate of pain in labor and the
plasma B-enorphin levels 24 hours later,
suggesting that B-endorphin plays an
analgesic role during labor and delivery.
Also found was a positive correlation
between the levels of B-endorphin at
delivery and the woman's attitude toward
her pregnancy at 36 weeks gestation. It
is possible that the rapid decline in the
levels of B-endorphin after delivery may
cause a B-endorphin "withdrawal" which
could be a cause of "post-natal blues,"
but then results neither prove nor
disprove this hypothesis.

436. Newton, Michael.
1977 "Woman, Wife, Mother: Meeting Sexual
and Emotional Needs During Pregnancy."
FAMILY HEALTH 9(10):15-16.

437. Newton, Niles.
1963 "Emotions and Pregnancy." In:
PRENATAL CARE. (M.E. Davis, ed.) New
York: Hoeber. pp. 639-667.

438. _____ .
1976 BIRTH RITUALS IN CROSS-CULTURAL
PERSPECTIVE: SOME PRACTICAL
APPLICATIONS. Proceedings of the 9th
International Congress of Anthropology
and Ethnology Sciences, Section on
Status of Female: Reproduction in World
Anthropology. The Hague, Netherlands.

439. Newton, N., and M. Newton.
1972 CHILDBIRTH IN CROSS CULTURAL
PERSPECTIVE. In: MODERN PERSPECTIVES IN
PSYCHO-OBSTETRICS. New York:
Brunner-Mazel.

440. Nilsson, Ake.
1970 "Para-Natal Emotional Adjustment. A
Prospective Investigation of 165 Women.
PART I. A GENERAL ACCOUNT OF BACKGROUND
VARIABLES, Attitudes Towards Childbirth,
and an Appreciation of Psychiatric
Morbidity." ACTA. PSYCHIAT. SCAND.,
SUPPL. 220:9-61.

441. Nilsson, Ake, and Per-Erik Almgren.
1970 "Para-natal Emotional Adjustment. A
Prospective Investigation of 165 Women.
Part II. The Influence of Background
Factors, Psychiatric History, Parental
Relations, and Personality
Characteristics." ACTA. PSYCHIAT.
SCAND., SUPPL. 220:63-141.

442. Nilsson, A.; L. Kaij; and L. Jacobson.
1967 "Post-partum Mental Disorder in an
Unselected Sample. The Psychiatric
History." J. PSYCHOSOM. RES. 10:327-339.

443. _____.
    1967 "The Importance of the Unplanned
    Pregnancy." J. PSYCHOSOM. RES.
    10:341-347.

444. Nilsson, Ake; N. Uddenberg; and Per-Erik
    Almgren.
    1971 "Parental Relations and
    Identification in Women with Special
    Regard to Prenatal Emotional
    Adjustment." ACTA. PSYCHIAT. SCAND.
    47:57-81.

445. Noble, Dorinda N., and Adrianne K.
    Hamilton.
    1981 "Families Under Stress: Perinatal
    Social Work." HEALTH AND SOC. WORK
    6:28-35.

    7) Article describes how the social worker
    can: a) Facilitate communication between
    medical personnel and the family, assess
    the support available to the mother, and
    act as patient advocate with the
    hospital's business office; b) Minimize
    the stress of separation on the family;
    c) Promote infant-parent bonding; d) Help
    family members deal with their feelings;
    and e) Help family plan for the future,
    according to the infant's condition.

446. Normand, W.
    1967 "Post-partum Disorders." In:
    COMPREHENSIVE TEXTBOOK OF PSYCHIATRY.
    (A. Freedman and H. Kaplan, eds.)
    Baltimore: Williams and Wilkins.

447. Notman, Malkah T., and Carol Nadelson.
1980 "Reproductive Crises." In: WOMEN AND
PSYCHOTHERAPY: AN ASSESSMENT OF RESEARCH
AND PRACTICE. (Annette M. Brodsky and
Rachel T. Hare-Mustin, eds.) New York:
Guilford Press. pp. 307-338.

448. Nott, P.N.
1982 "Psychiatric Illness Following
Childbirth in Southampton - A Case
Register Study." PSYCHOL. MED.
12(3):557-561.

449. Nott, P.N., and S. Cutts.
1982 "Validation of the 30-Item General
Health Questionnaire in Postpartum
Women." PSYCHOL. MED. 12(2):409-413.

1) Point study. 2) Two hundred women from
five Southampton General Practices who
were between 8 and 14 weeks postpartum
were visited at home. 3) Each women was
given the 30-item General Health
Questionnaire (GHQ) and a standardized
psychiatric interview. 4) The G.H.Q.
scores indicated psychiatric "caseness"
(psychiatric disorder). 6) Slight
modification of the content and a raised
cut-off point of the G.H.Q. make it a
useful screening instrument for postpartum
psychiatric disorder.

450. Nott, P.N.; M. Franklin; C. Armitage; and
M.G. Gelder.
1976 "Hormonal Changes and Mood in the
Puerperium." BR. J. PSYCHIAT.
128:379-383.

1) Prospective. 2) 27 married women (13
primiparous) from an antenatal department
(17-32 years old) without psychiatric

disorders or medical complications within 6 weeks of delivery. 3) subjects interviewed and blood taken 3 times before delivery, in hospital, the day after delivery, on alternate days for the first week and thereafter at home every 3rd day for 5 to 10 weeks, always between 9 am and noon. 5) At the second interview an Eysenck Personality Inventory Form A (EPI) was given. At all interviews three measures of emotional disturbance were given: Wakefield Inventory; Pitt's Scale; and the Lorr and McNair Scale. 6) The predelivery estrogen levels were higher in those who were more irritable; the greater the drop in progesterone levels, the more likely the women were to rate themselves as depressed within 10 days, but the less likely they were to report sleep disturbances; and the lower the estrogen levels after the delivery, the more likely the sample reported sleep disturbances.

451. Nuckolls, Katherine B.; John Cassel; and Berton H. Kaplan.
     1972 "Psychosocial Assets, Life Crisis and the Prognosis of Pregnancy." AM. J. EPID. 95(5):431-441.

1) Prospective. 2) Tapps (Psychosocial Asset Score) questionnaire administered to all white primagravidas prior to 24th week of pregnancy at a large military hospital. Schedule of Recent Experience (Life Change Score) was mailed to subjects during 32nd week of their pregnancies. Medical records were reviewed to determine "complicated" or "normal" outcome of pregnancy. Study sample size was 170. 6) Neither multiple life changes nor variations in psychosocial assets were, in

themselves, related to complications of
pregnancy. However, considering these
variables together, it was found that if
the Life Change Score was high both before
and during pregnancy, women scoring high
in favorable psychosocial assets had only
one third the complication rate of women
with low TAPPS scores.

452. Oakley, A.
1980 WOMEN CONFINED: TOWARDS A SOCIOLOGY
OF BIRTH. Oxford: Martin Robertson and
Co.

453. Obeyesekere, G.
1963 "Pregnancy Cravings (Dola-Duka) in
Relation to Social Structure and
Personality in a Sinhalese Village."
AM. ANTHRO. 65:323-342.

454. O'Hara, Kenshiro.
1973 "Mental Disorders and Mother-Child
Relationships: A View of Mother-Child
Double Suicide." CLIN. PSYCHIAT.
(Tokyo) 15(12):1271-1278.

455. O'Hara, Michael W.; L.P. Rehm; and S.B.
Cambell.
1982 "Predicting Depressive
Symptomatology: Cognitive-Behavioral
Models and Postpartum Depression." J.
ABNORMAL PSYCHOL. 91(6):457-461.

1) Prospective study. 2) Volunteers from
public and private prenatal clinics, 170
women in second trimester. 3) Beck
Depression Scale administered in 2nd
trimester and approximately 3 months
postpartum. 5) The Beck Depression
Inventory used primarily. 6) Delivery
stress related inversely to postpartum

depression levels. The best predictor of postpartum depression was the depression level during pregnancy. 7) Authors suggest periodic screenings to alert physicians to the patients with risk of developing problems in postpartum adjustment.

456. O'Hara, Michael W., et al.
1983 "Postpartum Depression: A Role for Social Network and Life Stress Variables." J. NERV. MENT. 171(6):336-341.

1) Prospective. 2) 30 selected from a public obstetric clinic (and part of a larger longitudinal study). 3) Mothers interviewed 17 weeks before birth and 10 weeks following, on average. 5) Beck Depression Index and Schedule for Affective Disorders and Schizophrenia. 6) A relationship between stressful life events and depression was supported. The Social Readjustment Rating Scale for life events since the beginning of pregnancy and the Stressful Circumstances Scale differentiated the two groups. Authors stress the importance of the marital relationship and to a lesser degree the role of a confidant during the postpartum period.

457. O'Hara, M.W.; D.J. Neunaber; and E.M. Zekoski.
1984 "Prospective Study of Postpartum Depression: Prevalence, Course, and Predictive Factors." J. ABNORMAL PSYCHOL. 93(2):158-171.

1) Prospective. 2) 99 women were recruited during prenatal visits to a

public obstetrics and gynecology clinic
and two private practices. The women were
followed from the second trimester of
pregnancy to 6 months postpartum. 3) Beck
Diagnostic Inventory (BDI), Self-Control
Questionnaire, Attributional Style
Questionnaire, and the Pilkonis Life
Events Schedule. A follow-up diagnostic
interview was completed at 9 weeks
postpartum and 6 months postpartum. 4) No
definition of postpartum depression was
given, but a model of postpartum
depression was developed which posits that
dysfunctional ways of thinking, a personal
and family history of depression, and the
experience of high levels of stressful
life events increase the likelihood of
depression following childbirth. 5) The
Beck Diagnostic Inventory was used as the
primary measure of depression. 6)
Depression severity decreased steadily
from the second trimester until 9 weeks
postpartum. Approximately 9% of women
during pregnancy and 12% of women during
the postpartum period were diagnosed
(using the RDC) as having a major or minor
depression. A model of depression was
constructed to account for both postpartum
depression symptomatology and the syndrome
of postpartum depression.

458. Oltman, J.E., and S. Friedman.
1965 "Trends in Postpartum Illness." AM.
J. PSYCHIAT. 122:328-329.

459. Omini, C., et al.
     1979 "Prostacyclin in Pregnant Human
          Uterus." PROSTOGLAND. 17:113-120.

460. Ordway, M.D., and A.M. McIntire.
     1942 "Mental Disorders Associated with
          Pregnancy and the Puerperium." NEW.
          ENGL. J. MED. 226(25):969-974.

461. Osterman, E.
     1963 "Des Etats psychopathologiques du
          postpartum." ACTA. PSYCHIAT. SCAND.
          39:190-192. SUPP. 169.

462. _____.
     1963 "Les Etats psychopathologiques du
          postpartum." L'ENCEPHALE 5:385-420.

463. Ostwald, P.F., and P.F. Regan III.
     1957 "Psychiatric Disorders Associated
          with Childbirth." J. NERV. MENT. DIS.
          125:153-165.

464. Paffenbarger, Ralph S., Jr.
     1964 "Epidemiological Aspects of
          Parapartum Mental Illness." BR. J.
          PREV. AND SOC. MED. 18(4):189-195.

465. Paffenbarger, Ralph S., Jr., and L.J.
          McCabe.
     1966 "The Effect of Obstetric and
          Perinatal Events on Risk of Mental
          Illness in Women of Childbearing Age."
          AM. J. PUBL. HEALTH 56:400-407.

466. Paffenbarger, Ralph S., Jr.; C.H.
          Steinmetz; B.G. Pooler; and R.T. Hyde.
     1961 "The Picture Puzzle of the Postpartum
          Psychoses." J. CHRON. DIS. 13:161-173.

467. Parfitt, D.N.
     1934 "Psychoses Associated with
     Childbirth." J. MENT. SCI. 80:43-57.

468. Parlee, M.B.
     1976 "Social Factors in the Psychology of
     Menstruation, Birth, and Menopause."
     PRIMARY CARE 3(3):477-490.

469. _____.
     1978 "Psychological Aspects of
     Menstruation, Childbirth, and Menopause:
     An Overview with Suggestions for Further
     Research." In: THE PSYCHOLOGY OF WOMEN:
     FUTURE DIRECTIONS OF RESEARCH. (V.
     Sherman and F. Denmark, eds.) New York:
     Psychological Dimensions.

470. Pascal, J.M., and J.A. Earp.
     1984 "The Effects of Mothers' Social
     Support and Life Changes on the
     Stimulation of Their Children in the
     Home..." AM. J. PUBLIC HEALTH
     74(4):358-360. (also see :310-312)

471. Paschall, N., et al.
     1976 "Personality Factors and Postpartum
     Adjustment." PRIMARY CARE 3(4):
     741-750.

472. Pasnau, R.
     1975 "Psychiatry and
     Obstetrics-Gynecology: Report of a
     Five-Year Experience in Psychiatry
     Liaison." In: CONSULTATION-LIASION
     PSYCHIATRY. (R. Pasnau, ed.) New York:
     Grune and Stratton.

473. Pasquarelli, B.
1952 "Psychotic Reactions to Pregnancy."
In: MANIC-DEPRESSIVE PSYCHOSIS AND
ALLIED CONDITIONS. (L. Bellak, ed.) New
York: Grune and Stratton. pp 206-219.

474. Paul, O.P.
1974 "A Study of Puerperal Psychosis." J.
INDIAN MED. ASSOC. 63(3):84-89.

1) Retrospective. 2) Cases included in
the study were all those in which
puerperal psychosis started within six
weeks after childbirth and were admitted
to St. James University Hospital, Leeds.
One hundred cases were identified. 4) The
postpartum period was defined as birth to
six weeks. 5) Author accepted the
diagnosis of the attending physician. 6)
Sixty percent of cases were in the age
group of 20-30. Affective disorder,
particularly depressive illness, was more
common in the higher age groups while
schizophrenia predominated in the younger
age group. Fifty percent of the cases
were primiparae. Twenty-seven percent
showed a positive history of past mental
illness. Extramarital conception,
unwanted pregnancy, condition of the
infant, and family history showed no
correlation with postpartum mental
illness. In light of the results, it is
the author's opinion that "the various
mental illnesses, called puerperal
psychosis, are not different from those
occuring in the general population. so
puerperal psychosis is a blanket term,
used for a variety of psychiatric illness
occuring during the puerperium."

475. Pauleikhoff, B.
1964 SEELISCHE STORUNGEN IN DER
SCHWANGERSCHAFT UND NACH DER GEBURT.
Stuttgart: Enke.

476. Paykel, E.S.; E.M. Emms; J. Fletcher; and
E.S. Rassaby.
1980 "Life Events and Social Support in
Puerperal Depression." BR. J. PSYCHIAT.
136:339-346.

1) Point study. 2) 120 caucasian women
attending postnatal clinics at two London
hospitals. 3) One private interview at
about 6 weeks postpartum provided
information on personal history,
pregnancy, delivery, recent life events
and recent depressive symptoms. 5) Rating
instruments were the Raskin Three Area
Depression Scale, Interview for Recent
Life Events, and Semi-Structured Interview
for Personal History and Background
Information. 6) A 20% prevalence of mild
clinical depression was found in 120 women
assessed at about 6 weeks postpartum. The
factor most strongly associated with this
was occurrence of recent stressful life
events. Overall, findings indicate the
importance of social stress in puerperal
depression.

477. Paykel, E.S.; J.K. Myers; M. Dienelt; G.L.
Klerkman; J.J. Lindenthal; and M.P.
Pepper.
1969 "Life Events and Depression. A
Controlled Study." ARCH. GEN. PSYCHIAT.
21:753-760.

478. Peuteuil, P.A.; M. Lyvonnet; D.
     Klopfenstein; P. Safati; and B.
     Zurlinden.
     1972 "Interet d'une consultation de
     psychosexologie en
     gynecologie-obstetrique." JOURNAL DE
     MEDECINE DE BESANCON 8:329-334.

479. Phillipson-Price, Adrienne.   ,
     1982 "Expectancy and the Relationship of
     Postpartum Affect." DISS. ABSTR.
     McGill University.

     1) Prospective. 2) 30 primaparas mothers
     from birthing centers. 3) Pretested on
     labor and delivery expectation and post
     tested (two days postpartum). 5) Labor
     and Delivery Expectation Scale; Experience
     Scale. 6) Mothers who viewed their labor
     and delivery process as more positive than
     they had anticipated reported a more
     positive "mood" and a low "distress" level
     postpartum; conversely, if the birth
     process was more negative than the mothers
     had anticipated, the "mood" scores were low
     and "distress" levels high.

480. Piker, P.
     1938 "Psychoses Complicating Childbirth."
     AM. J. OBSTET. & GYNEC. 35:901-909.

481. Pillsbury, Barbara L.K.
     1978 "Doing the Month, Confinement and
     Convalescence of Chinese Women After
     Childbirth." SOC. SCI. MED. 12:11-22.

     1) Ethnographic. 2) Data were gathered in
     interviews with laypersons and physicians
     from The People's Republic of China and
     with laypersons, physicians, and
     herbalists in Taiwan. 6) Author describes

the practices of "doing the month" which
persist in China and Taiwan despite the
increased accessibility of Western medical
facilities. "Doing the month," the
rituals surrounding childbirth, are
analyzed first from the ethnomedical folk
perspective, then from the logic of
classical Chinese medicine, and finally,
from the Western medical and nutritional
framework. A direct relationship between
familial support and mental health during
the postpartum is declared. "This extra
attention their families and social
networks show them while doing the month
seems, in fact to preclude Chinese women
from experiencing postpartum depression as
understood and so taken for granted by
Americans--despite the fact that the same
biological factors are operative for women
of both cultural backgrounds. Neither the
Chinese translation of the term
'postpartum depression' nor the concept,
itself makes much sense to the majority of
my informants. 'You would just feel
disappointed,' explained one of them,
'Only if each time it is a girl, because
then you know the family is not
pleased'"(p. 18).

482. Pines, Dinora.
1972 "Pregnancy and Motherhood:
Interaction Between Fantasy and
Reality." BR. J. MED. PSYCHOL.
45(4):333-343.

483. Piscicelli, Umberto.
1972 "L'igiene mentale nella
psicoprofilassi al parto indolore."
IGIENE MENTALE 16(1):254-259.

484. Pitt, Brice M.N.
      1966 "A Study of Emotional Disturbance
      Associated with Childbearing." M.D.
      THESIS, UNIVERSITY OF LONDON.

485. _____.
      1968 "Atypical Depression Following
      Childbirth." BR. J. PSYCHIAT.
      114:1325-1335.

486. _____.
      1972 "Neurotic (or Atypical) Depression
      Following Childbirth." PSYCHOSOMATIC
      MEDICINE. In: OBSTETRICS AND GYNECOLOGY.
      THIRD INTERNATIONAL CONGRESS. Basel:
      Karger.

487. _____.
      1973 "Maternity Blues." BR. J. PSYCHIAT.
      122:431-433.

488. _____.
      1975 "Psychological Reactions to
      Childbirth." PROC. R. SOC. MED.
      68(4):223-224.

489. _____.
      1975 "Psychiatric Illness Following
      Childbirth." BR. J. PSYCHIAT. 9:409-15.

1) Summary. 7) For treatment Pitt
suggests prevention by an interview and
assessment of the mother-to-be during an
early prenatal visit. Patients more
susceptible to mental illness should be
screened. Also warning signs such as
lower abdominal pain, vaginal discharge,
and "pathological anxiety" should be
viewed as possible precusors to
depression. When depression is exhibited
most patients should be treated in the

hospital with their baby, so as to be away
from stress at home. He suggests
psychotherapy as the most effective form
of treatment and, when necessary, in
combination with antidepressives and
tranquilizers.

490. _____.
1975 "Psychiatric Illness Following
Childbirth." BR. J. PSYCHIAT. SPEC. NO.
9:409-415.

491. Playfair, H.R., and J.L. Gowers.
1981 "Depression Following Childbirth--A
Search for Predictive Signs." JR. COLL.
GEN. PRAC. 31:201.

492. Pleschette, N., et al.
1956 "A Study of Anxieties During
Pregnancy, Labor, and Early, and Late
Puerperium." BULL. NY. ACAD. MED.
32:436-455.

493. Polonio, P., and M. Figueiredo.
1955 "On the Structure of Mental Disorders
Associated with Childbearing." MSCHR.
PSYCHIAT. NEUROL. 130:304-319.

494. Power, T.G., and R.D. Parke.
1984 "Social Network Factors and the
Transition to Parenthood." SEX ROLES
10(11):949-972.

495. Protheroe, C.
1969 "Puerperal Psychoses: A Long-Term
Study 1927-1961." BRIT. J. PSYCHIAT.
115:9-30.

496. Prothro, E.T.
     1961 CHILD REARING IN THE LEBANON.
          Cambridge, Mass.: Harvard University
          Press.

497. Pugh, T.F.; B.K. Jerath; W.M. Schmidt; and
     R.B. Reed.
     1963 "Rates of Mental Disease Related to
          Childbearing." NEW ENGL. J. MED.
          268(22):1224-1228.

498. Pye, Carol J.
     1981 "Postpartum Depression: A Prospective
          Multivariate Study of Normal Primiparous
          Women." DISS. ABSTR. INT. Queen's
          University (Canada).

499. Quijano, E.C., and G. Cobliner.
     1983 "Post-partum Depression in
          Adolescents." J. ADOLESCENT HEALTH CARE
          4(3):213.

1) Point-study. 2) Test administered to
40 adolescents (12-17 years old). 3)
Subjects tested within one year of
delivery (2-12 months) and elected from a
teen pregnancy clinic. 5) Beck Depression
Scale. 6) 15 girls (38%) of the 40
experienced postpartum depression
symptoms. One girl showed signs of
possible suicide but none made
self-destructive attempts. The depressed
girls were significantly younger and had a
significantly lower gynecologic age. All
depressed girls had unintended
pregnancies. 12 of the 25 nondepressed
had intended pregnancies. Although it was
not significant, the depressed girls
seemed to have poorer relationships with
their mothers.

500. Radloff, L.
     1975 "Sex Differences in Depression. The
     Effects of Occupation and Marital
     Status." SEX ROLES 1:249-269.

501. Railton, I.E.
     1961 "The Use of Corticoids in Postpartum
     Depression." J. AM. MED. WOMEN'S ASSOC.
     16:450-452.

502. Rees, W., and S. Lutkins.
     1971 "Parental Depression Before and After
     Childbirth." J. ROY. COLL. GEN. PRAC.
     21:26-31.

503. Reich, T., and G. Winokur.
     1970 "Postpartum Psychosis in Patients
     with Manic Depressive Disease." J.
     NERV. AND MENT. DIS. 151:60-69.

504. Resnich, Phillip J.
     1969 "Child Murder by Parents: A
     Psychiatric Review of Filicide." AM. J.
     PSYCHIAT. 126:326-334.

505. _____.
     1970 "Murder of the Newborn: A Psyciatric
     Review of Neonaticide." AM. J.
     PSYCHIAT. 126:1414-1420.

506. Rey, J.H.; U. Nicholson-Bailey; and A.
     Trappl.
     1957 "Endocrine Activity in Psychiatric
     Patients with Menstrual Disorders." BR.
     MED. J. 1:843-850.

507. Rich, Adrienne.
     1976 OF WOMAN BORN: MOTHERHOOD AS
     EXPERIENCE AND INSTITUTION. New York:
     Norton.

508. Richman, Naomi.
1976 "Depression in Mothers of Preschool Children." J. CHILD PSYCHOL. AND PSYCHIAT. (Oxford) 17(1):75-78.

509. Ricksher, Charles.
1909 "A Study of the Psychoses Beginning in the Puerperal States." BOSTON M. & S. J. 161(5):142.

510. Rigden, A.
1906 "The Insanity of Childbirth." BR. MED. J. 2:1253-1257.

511. Ripping, L.H.
1877 DIE GEISTESSTORUNGEN DER SCHWANGEREN, WOCHNERINNEN UND SAUGENDEN. Stuttgart.

512. Robertson, Joann M.
1976 "The Abusive Parent: A Different Perspective." CANADA'S MENTAL HEALTH 24(4):18-19.

513. _____.
1980 "A Treatment Model for Postpartum Depression." CANADA'S MENTAL HEALTH 28(2):16-17.

1) Commentary. 4) Anxiety, sleeplessness, loss of self, and subjective descriptions of depression. 5) Self-identification. 7) Depressed women are offered an environment to share their feelings with other women and are counselled by volunteers who experienced postpartum depression difficulties. Daily telephone conversations are held between counselors and victims for as long as necessary. Information meetings for fathers are held once a month and individual counseling given if needed.

514. Robin, A.
1962 "Psychological Changes of Normal
Parturition." PSYCHIAT. QUART.
36:129-150.

515. Robinson, A. Leyland.
1933 "The Effect of Reproducton upon
Insanity." J. OBST. GYNEC. BR. EMP.
40(1):39-66.

516. Robinson, St, and Ja Young.
1982 "Screening for Depression and Anxiety
in the Postnatal Period--Acceptance or
Rejection of a Subsequent Treatment
Offer." AUST. NZ. J. PSYCHIATRY
16(2):47-51.

1) Point-study. 2) 288 women attending
Community Baby Health Center at 6-8 weeks
postpartum. 3) Given Leeds Scale
(Self-Rating Survey) at the clinic visit.
If scores were positive for depression or
anxiety, a 2nd Leeds Scale was completed 6
months postpartum. 5) Leeds scale. If
positive, a psychiatric consultation was
offered. This consisted of a traditional
one-hour interview with a psychiatrist
which focused on physical and
psychological concomitants of depression,
present for at least 2 weeks. Formal
diagnosis of clinical depression followed
if perceived by psychiatrist. 6)
Incidence of depression at 6-8 weeks
postpartum was 6% and considered lower
than on previous comparable Self-Rating
Scales. 7) Psychiatric consultation
and/or treatment offered women suspected
of postpartum anxiety or depression.
Author comments on feasibility of
introducing mental health assessment as a
routine procedure in baby health centers.

517. Robson, Kay M., and R. Kumar.
     1980 "Delayed Onset of Maternal Affection
     After Childbirth." BR. J. PSYCHIAT.
     13:347-353.

518. Robson, Kay M.; H.A. Brant; and R. Kumar.
     1981 "Maternal Sexuality During First
     Pregnancy and After Childbirth." J.
     OBSTET. GYNAEC. 88:882-889.

519. Rogers, S.C.
     1965 "Depression Following Childbirth."
     PRACTITIONER 194:257-260.

520. Romer, H.
     1941 "Zur Diagnose und Therapie der
     Puerperalpsychosen." MED. KLIN. 16:1.

521. Rosberg, Jack, and Bertram P. Karon.
     1959 "A Direct Analytic Contribution to
     the Understanding of Post-partum
     Psychosis." PSYCHIAT. QUART.
     33(2):296-304.

522. Rosenwald, George C., and Marshall W.
     Stonehill.
     1972 "Early and Late Postpartum
     Illnesses." PSYCHOSOM. MED.
     34(2):129-137.

1) Retrospective. 2) 26 case histories
selected from mothers admitted to a mental
health center. 3) The subjects were
divided into two groups according to the
date of admission: 12-within the first
postpartum 5 weeks, and 14-after 2 and 1/2
months but not yet 15 months postpartum.
Eight variables were studied: chief
complaint, personal history, history of
the illness, social history, marital
history, sexual history, play history, and

work history. 6) The following hypothesis was tested and confirmed: mothers hospitalized early were overwhelmed chiefly by the birth process, while mothers hospitalized later collapsed under the emotional burdens related to child care. In addition the birth event is especially difficult for mothers with schizoid traits; later childrearing tasks are taxing for narcissistic women.

523. Roten, E.
1975 "Subconscious Anxiety About Children as Cause of Pains During Pregnancy and Postpartum Depression with Presentation of 12 Cases." ZEITSCHRIFT FUR PSYCHOSOMATISCHE MEDIZIN UND PSYCHOANALYSE 21(2):197.

524. Roth, Nathan.
1975 "The Mental Content of Puerperal Psychoses." AM. J. PSYCHOTHERAPY 29(2):204-211.

525. Rozdilsky, Mary Lou, and Barbara Banet.
1975 WHAT NOW? A HANDBOOK FOR NEW PARENTS. New York: Charles Scribner's Sons. pp 16-22.

526. Rubin, R.
1967 "Puerperal Change." NURS. OUTLOOK 9:753.

527. Ruddock E.H.
1886 THE LADY'S MANUAL OF HOMEOPATHIC TREATMENT. Homeopathic Publishing Co. pp. 215-217.

118

528. Ryle, A.
1961 "The Psychological Disturbances
Associated with 345 Pregnancies in 137
Women." J. MENT. SCI. 107:279-286.

529. St. Claire-Vernan, J.
1968 "Some Problems Connected with
Postnatal Depression." MIDWIFE HEALTH
VISITOR 4:373-375.

530. Sandler, Merton, ed.
1978 MENTAL ILLNESS IN PREGNANCY AND THE
PUERPERIUM. London: Oxford Univ.
Press.

531. Sandy, W.C.
1913 "Psychoses Associated with
Childbearing." J. M. SOC. NEW JERSEY
10:230-232.

532. Sargent, Carolyn F.
1980 THE CULTURAL CONTEXT OF THERAPEUTIC
CHOICE: OBSTETRICAL CARE DECISIONS
AMOUNG THE BARIBA OF BENIN. Hingham,
Mass.: Klumer Academic Press

533. Sargent, Susan Pickman.
1977 "Prepartum Maternal Attitudes,
Neonatal Characteristics, and
Post-partum Adaptation of Mother and
Infant." DISS. ABSTR. INTL.
38(4-B):1903-1904.

534. Saucier, J.F.
1972 "Correlates of the Long Post-partum
Taboo: A Cross-Cultural Study." C.
ANTHRO. 13:238-266.

535. Saunders, E.R.
     1929 "Association of Psychoses with the
     Puerperium." AM. J. PSYCHIAT.
     8:669-680.

536. Savage, G.H.
     1875 "Observations on the Insanity of
     Pregnancy and Childbirth." GUY'S HOSP.
     REP. 20:83-117.

537. _____.
     1888-1889 "Septic Puerperal Insanity."
     PROC. M. SOC. London 12:90-100.

538. _____.
     1896 "Prevention and Treatment of Insanity
     of Pregnancy and the Puerperal Period."
     LANCET 1:164-165.

539. Schachter, J.; J. Kerr; and F. Wimberly.
     1974 "Racial Differences in Newborn Heart
     Rate Level." PSYCHOPHYSIOLOGY
     11(2):220.

1) Prospective. 2) Newborn offspring born
to schizophrenic mothers (52 white and 47
black) were studied. 3) Swaddled newborns
were presented with repeated auditory
clicks for a three and one-half
interfeeding period on the second and
again on the third postnatal day. During
each 20 minutes of the session, the
average R-R interval period was calculated
for 10 twenty-second epochs during which
time no effective stimulus occurred. 4)
The postpartum was defined as the second
and third days. 6) Black babies were
found to have higher heart-rate levels
than white babies. Heart-rate levels for
the first 20 minutes of each session
showed no association with: a) Level of

maternal depression or anxiety during
pregnancy; b) parity; c) Gestational age;
d) Birth weight; or e) Level of maternal
medication during delivery.

540. Schearer, M.L.; R.T. Davidson; and S.M.
Finch.
1967 "The Sex Ratio of Offspring Born to
State Hospitalized Schizophrenic Women."
J. PSYCHIAT. RES. 5:349-350.

541. Schmidt, H.J.
1943 "The Use of Progesterone in the
Treatment of Postpartum Psychosis." J.
AM. MED. ASSOC. 121(3):190-192.

542. Schopf, J.; C. Bryois; M. Jonquiera; and
P.K. Le.
1984 "On the Nosology of Severe
Psychiatric Postpartum
Disorders--Results of a Catamnestic
Investigation." EUR ARCH PS
234(1):54-63. (Swiss)

543. Schorer, C.E.
1972 "Gestational Schizophrenia." CANAD.
PSYCHIAT. ASSOC. J., SUPPL. 17: 259-263.

544. Schreuder-Hoekstra, J.C.E.
1983 "Post-Natal (-Partum) Depression,
Illness or Disease?" J. OF
PSYCHOSOMATIC OBSTETRICS AND GYNAECOLOGY
2-I:56-58.

545. Schroder, P.
1936 "Uber wochbettspsychosen und beutige
Diagnostik." ALLG. ZTSCHR. FUR
PSYCHIAT. 104:177-207.

546. Schuerman, John R.
1972 "Marital Interaction and Posthospital
Adjustment." SOCIAL CASEWORK
53:163-172.

547. Schwengenheuer, J.
1953 "Uber Generationspsychosen." ARCHIV
FUR PSYCHIAT. ZEITSCHRIFT NEUROLOGIC,
BD. 190:150-165.

548. Sclare, B.A.
1955 "Psychiatric Aspects of Pregnancy and
Childbirth." PRACTITIONER 175:146-154.

549. Seager, C.P.
1960 "A Controlled Study of Post Partum
Mental Illness." J. MENT. SCI.
106:214-230.

550. Sears, R.R.; E.E. MacCoby; and H. Levin.
1957 PATTERNS OF CHILD REARING. Evanston,
ILL.: Row Peterson.

551. Seashore, Marjorie J., et al.
1973 "The Effects of Denial of Early
Mother-Infant Interactions on Maternal
Self-Confidence." J. PERSONALITY AND
SOCIAL PSYCHOLOGY 26(3):369-378.

552. Seiden, A.
1978 "The Sense of Mastery in the
Childbirth Experience." In: THE WOMAN
PATIENT: MEDICAL AND PSYCHOLOGICAL
INTERFACES. (M. Notman and C. Nadelson,
eds.) New York: Plenum Press.

553. Seidenberg, R., and L. Harris.
1949 "Prenatal Symptoms in Post Partum
Psychotic Reactions." PSYCHIAT. QUART.
23:715-719.

554. Seitz, Pauline M., and Louise H. Warrick.
     1974 "Perinatal Death: The Grieving
     Mother." AM. J. NURSING
     74(11):2028-2033.

555. Semenov, S.F., et al.
     1976 "Clinical Features and Problems in
     the Differential Diagnosis of
     Schizophrenic Psychoses Developing After
     Delivery." ZH. NEUROPATOL. PSIKHIATR.
     76(5):741-747. (Eng. Abs.)

     1) Retrospective. 2) This was a follow-up
     study of 75 schizophrenic patients
     observed during the puerperium. 6) A
     recurrent psychosis and an attack-like
     progressive psychosis were distinguished.
     Some differential diagnostic criteria are
     given so as to differentiate recurrent
     schizophrenia from somatogenic and
     infectious psychoses.

556. Seward, Elizabeth M.
     1972 "Preventing Postpartum Psychosis."
     AM. J. NURS. 72(3):520-523.

557. Shah, D.K.; N.N. Wig; and Salman Akttar.
     1971 "Status of Postpartum Mental Illness
     in Psychiatric Nosology: A Study of 102
     Cases." INDIAN J. PSYCHIAT. 13:14-20.

     1) Retrospective. 2) One hundred two
     cases of psychiatric disorders subsequent
     to childbirth attending the Psychiatric
     Clinic of Postgraduate Institute of
     Medical Education and Research,
     Chandigarh, from 1964 to 1969, were
     reviewed. 4) The postpartum period was
     defined as the 42 days following
     parturition. 5) Classifications follow
     those set by the World Health Organization

in 1965, ICD-8. This study covers neurotic
reactions associated with childbearing as
well. Diagnostic categories covered were
schizophrenia, affective psychosis, acute
organic brain syndrome, and neurosis. 6)
The incidence of postpartum psychiatric
disorders is two of the total clinic
population. (Author does not feel this is
a comparative statistic, however,)
Twenty-four and three/tenths percent had a
personal history and 23.5% had a family
history of previous psychiatric disorders.
More than 50% had stressful situations
concurrent to labor; 89% were typical of
the standard category assigned to them.
Parity of the patient and sex of the child
delivered were of no significance. Author
feels "These observations clearly indicate
that there is a high degree of genetic
loading, marked susceptibility to stress,
low incidence of atypical clinical
presentation and apparently no
significance of specific factors related
to child bearing."

558. Shereshefsky, P.M., and L.J. Yarrow.
     1973 PSYCHOLOGICAL ASPECTS OF A FIRST
         PREGNANCY AND EARLY POSTNATAL
         ADAPTATION. New York: Raven Press.

559. Sherman, Julia A.
     1973 ON THE PSYCHOLOGY OF WOMEN: A SURVEY
         OF EMPIRICAL STUDIES. Springfield,
         Ill.: Charles C. Thomas.

560. Sichel, J.P., and R. Chepfer.
     1974 "Some Possible Connections Between
         Normal Deliveries and Postpartum
         Psychosis." EVOLUTION PSYCHIATRIQUE
         39(3):643-662.

561. Siegenthaler, E.
1898 "Beitrag zu den puerperalpsychosen."
JAHRB. F. PSYCHIAT. 17:87-143.

562. Silva, Lalitha Da, and Eve C. Johnstone.
1981 "A Follow-Up Study of Severe
Puerperal Psychiatric Illness." BR. J.
PSYCHIAT. 139:346-354.

563. Silvestro, J.R., and A.R. Fosson.
1982 "Attitudes of Postpartum Mothers
Concerning Children and Child-Rearing."
SOUTH MED. J. 75(10):1171-1176.

564. Sim, M.
1963 "Abortion and the Psychiatrist." BR.
MED. J. 2:145-148.

565. Simon, A.
1951 "Mental Illness Associated with
Pregnancy." M. BULL. UNIV. CALIFORNIA
M. CENTER 2:646-663.

566. Siris, Samuel G.; Harvey R. Chertoff; and
James M. Perel.
1979 "Rapid-Cycling Affective Disorder
During Imipramine Treatment: A Case
Report." AM. J. PSYCHIAT.
136(3):341-342.

1) Clinical interview. 2) This is
basically a case study of a new mother
suffering from what was viewed as a
genetically inherited depression. 6)
Authors found that after this woman had
taken imipramine for depression triggered
by a conflict over breast feeding, she
underwent 15 major mood changes between a
depressed state and either euthymia or
hypomania over a 10-week period. They
found her to react favorably to lithium

which was expected. Although a single
case is inconclusive, the authors
recommend additional research. 7) Authors
encourage identification of similar
patients and suggest lithium in treatment
of unipolar depression.

567. Skalickova, O., and P. Pavlovsky.
     1968 "Deaths Related to Psychosis in
       Gestation." CESKOSLOVENSKA PSYCHIATRIE
       (Prague) 64(3):154-158.

     1) Retrospective. 2) Women who died from
     psychoses due to gestation from 1962 to
     1966. The records were obtained from the
     ministry of public health. There were 11
     cases of self-killing during this period.
     5) Author relied on the diagnosis of the
     attending physician. 6) The most frequent
     symptomatology was anxious-depressive.
     The most frequent cause of death was a
     jump from a window; the most frequent
     period, the end of the second and the
     beginning of the third week after
     parturition. Most of the women suffered
     from some metabolic disorders in the sense
     of "gestosis" or another disease.

568. Skottowe, Ian.
     1942 "Mental Disorders in Pregnancy and
       the Puerperium." PRACTITIONER
       148:157-163.

569. Slater, Eliot, and Martin Roth.
     1969 CLINICAL PSYCHIATRY. 3RD EDITION.
       Baltimore: The Williams and Wilkins Co.
       904 pp.

570. Smalldon, J.L.
1940 "A Survey of Mental Illness
Associated with Pregnancy and
Childbirth." AM. J. PSYCHIAT.
97:80-101.

571. Smith, B.
1934 "Psychoses Associated with
Pregnancy." J. KANSAS MED. SOC.
35:203-209.

572. Smith-Rosenberg, Carol.
1972 "The Hysterical Woman: Sex Roles and
Role Conflict in Century America."
SOCIAL RES. 39(4):652-678.

573. Smoller, Bruce, and Alfred B. Lewis, Jr.
1977 "A Psychological Theory of Child
Abuse." PSYCHIATR. QUARTERLY
49(1):38-44.

574. Sneddon, Joan, and R.J. Kerry.
1980 "Puerperal Psychosis." BR. J.
PSYCHIAT. 136:520.

575. Snyder, S.
1978 "The Opiate Receptor and
Morphine-Like Peptides in the Brain."
AM. J. PSYCHIAT. 135:645-652.

576. Sosa, Roberto; John Kennell; Marshall
Klaus; Steven Robertson; and Juan
Urrutia.
1980 "The Effect of a Supportive Companion
on Perinatal Problems, Lenght of Labor,
and Mother-Infant Interaction." NEW
ENGL. J. MED. 303(11):597-599.

577. Sostek, A.M.; J.W. Scanlon; and D.C.
     Abramson.
     1982 "Postpartum Contact and Maternal
     Confidence and Anxiety--A Confirmation
     of Short-Term Effects." INFANT BEH.
     5(4):323-329.

578. Srivastaia, Sahab Lai.
     1971 "Birth Rites: A Comparative Study."
     E. ANTHROPOL. 24(2):181-196.

579. Stahlie, T.D.
     1960 "Pregnancy and Childbirth in
     Thailand." TROP. GEOGR. MED. 2:127-137.

580. Stein, George; Frank Milton; Penny
     Bebbington; Keith Wood; and Alec Coppen.
     1976 "Relationship Between Mood
     Disturbances and Free Total Plasma
     Tryptophan in Postpartum Women." BR.
     MED. J. 2(6033):457.

1) Prospective. 2) Eighteen women in a
postnatal clinic participated in the
study. 3) Cohorts rated themselves daily
from 0-4 for each of the following five
symptoms: tearfulness, depression,
anxiety, appetite, and insomnia. On the
sixth day postpartum, a 30-ml fasting
blood sample was taken from each woman.
For comparison, groups of normal controls
and depressed in-patients were also
studied. Researchers measuring the levels
of free and total plasma tryptophan were
unaware of the psychiatric state of
patients at the time of measurement. 4)
The postpartum was defined as birth to
seven or eight days. 5) An average daily
score for each affective symptom was
calculated. The maximum daily total
affective score was 20. Patients were

then ranked in order of increasing
affective disturbance. Scores ranging
from 15-18 were diagnosed as having severe
depression. 6) Patients who scored in the
severe depression range had free plasma
tryptophan levels similar to the
depressive controls. Free plasma
tryptophan correlated significantly with
depression (p < 0.01) and also with the
total affective score (p < 0.05). The
other symptoms showed similar trends but
the correlation failed to reach
statistical significance. There was no
correlation between age and free plasma
tryptophan levels in any of the three
groups. Total plasma tryptophan did not
correlate with any of the clinical data
but was 33.5% higher in the controls.

581. Steinmann, I.
     1935 "Causes of Psychoses." ARCH. F.
     PSYCHIAT. 103:552-579.

582. Stephenson, R.; L. Huxel; and E.
     Harui-Walsh.
     1978 "From Wife to Mother: An Exploratory
     Study of Micronesian Post-Partum
     Practices." PRELIMINARY REPORT,
     UNPUBLISHED. University of Guam.

583. Stern, Edward S.
     1948 "The Media Complex: The Mother's
     Homicidal Wishes to Her Child." J.
     MENT. SCI. 94:321-331.

584. Stern, Gwen, and Laurence Kruckman.
     1983 "Multi-Disciplinary Perspectives on
     Post-Partum Depression: An
     Anthropological Critique." SOC. SCI.
     MED. 17(15):1027-1041.

1) Summary (with ethnographic studies).
4) A review of definitions with many
descriptive categories provided. 6) A
hypothesis is proposed that a relationship
exists between postpartum social
organization/mobilization and postpartum
depression. The experience of
"depression" in the U.S. may represent a
culture-bound syndrome resulting from the
lack of social structuring of the
postpartum events, social recognition of
the role transition for the new mother,
and instrumental support and aid for the
new mother.

585. Stevens, Barbara C.
1971 "Psychoses Associated with
Childbirth: A Demographic Survey Since
the Development of Community Care."
SOCIAL SCIENCE AND MEDICINE
5(6):527-543.

586. Stewart, D.B.
1967 "Complications of the Puerperium."
In: OBSTETRICS AND GYNAECOLOGY IN THE
TROPICS AND DEVELOPING COUNTRIES. (J.B.
Lawson, and D.B. Stewart, eds.) London:
Edward Arnold Publishers, Inc. pp.
242-252.

1) Instructional--directed toward other
physicians "in the field". 2) Author is
professor of obstetrics and gynaecology at
the University of the West Indies,
Jamaica. 4) The postpartum period is
defined as birth to six weeks. 6) "Many
women, particularly primigravidae,
experience a phase of depression--the
'maternity blues'--usually within the
first week after delivery." Peak
incidence for almost any type of

"definitive mental disorder" is about one
month postpartum. Puerperal schizophrenia
usually develops in people who have shown
these tendencies earlier, and it is
uncommon for any type of psychosis to
develop during the first 48 hours
postpartum. Author cautions "especially
in the tropics, it is most important to
remember that a confusional state in the
puerperium may be due to a severe
infection, or to toxic substances
contained in traditional medicines" and
"particularly among patients admitted in
an emergency, confused and apparently
irrational behaviour may result from the
sudden transition to totally unfamiliar
surroundings in hospital."

587. Strang, Victoria and Patricia Sullivan.
1985 "Body Image During Pregnancy and the
Postpartum Period." JOGN. 14(4):332-37.

1) Prospective. 2) Self-Administered
Attitude to Body Image Scale two and six
weeks postpartum to 63 multiparas and
primiparas mothers. 6) Majority of
mothers seemed to feel "slightly positive"
about their bodies at two and six weeks.
Multiparas felt more positive about their
postpartum image but perhaps the primiparas
may think it is reasonable to expect a
quick return of her body to its former
state, or, the multiparas were just not as
used in other research and is questioned
here; the ability to function could be the
"body" the mothers were concerned with
rather than their actual physical
appearance.

588. Strecker, E.A., and F.G. Ebaugh.
     1926 "Psychoses Occurring During the
          Puerperium." ARCH. NEUROL. PSYCHIAT.
          15:239-252.

589. Sugar, M.
     1977 "Prenatal Influences on
          Maternal-Infant Attachment." AM. J.
          ORTHOPSYCH. 47(3): 407-421.

590. Sugarman, Muriel.
     1977 "Paranatal Influences on
          Maternal-Infant Attachment." AM. J.
          ORTHOPSYCH. 47(3):407-419.

591. Swartz, Conrad M.
     1982 "Biologically Derived Depression and
          the Dexamethasone Suppression Test."
          COMPREHENSIVE PSYCHIATRY 23(4):339-344.

     1) Retrospective--prospective. 2) 14
     patients with Major Depressive Disorder
     (DSM III criteria). 3) Patients received
     1 mg of dexamethasone and blood samples
     taken 9 hours later. Serum analyzed and
     cortisol levels recorded. 4) Postpartum
     depression of onset between 2 days and 2
     weeks is seen as a biochemically derived
     depressive illness. It must have impaired
     mental functioning so that the patient was
     unable to meet the ordinary demands of
     life, and this state was distinctly
     different in character from the patient's
     customary state. 5) DSM-III criteria for
     Major Depressive Disorder. 6) Patients
     with abnormal cortisol suppression tests
     are more likely to show delusions or
     disorientation than those with normal
     tests.

592. Swift, C.R.
      1972 "Psychosis During the Puerperium
      Among Tanzanians." EAST AFRICAN MED. J.
      49(9):651-657.

593. Targum, Steven D.; Yolande D. Davenport;
      and Marian J. Webster.
      1979 "Postpartum Mania in Bipolar
      Manic-Depressive Patients Withdrawn from
      Lithium Carbonate." J. NERV. MENT. DIS.
      167(9):572-574.

594. Tauber, Margaret A.
      1974 "Postpartum Depression, Environmental
      Stress and Educational Aspiration."
      DISS. ABSTR. INTL. 34:6226, (12-B,p 1).

595. Taylor, M.A.
      1969 "Sex Ratios of Newborns: Associated
      with Prepartum and Postpartum
      Schizophrenia." SCIENCE 164:723-724.

596. _____.
      1970 "Sex Ratios of Newborns and
      Schizophrenia." SCIENCE 168:151-152.

597. Taylor, M.A., and R. Levine.
      1969 "Puerperal Schizophrenia: A
      Physiological Interaction Between Mother
      and Fetus." BIOL. PSYCHIAT. 43:396-409.

598. _____.
      1970 "The Interactive Effects of Maternal
      Schizophrenia and Offspring Sex." BIOL.
      PSYCHIAT. 2:279-284.

599. Telles, Cynthia A.
     1982 "Psychological and Physiological
     Adaption to Pregnancy and Childbirth in
     Low-income Hispanic Women." DISS.
     ABSTR. Boston University.

     1) Retrospective. 2) 110 women selected
     from birthing centers. 3) Sample was
     interviewed in the postnatal period and
     twice in the postpartum; medical records
     were reviewed. 5) Premenstrual Tension
     Scale, Cultural Awareness and Loyalty
     Scale, Personality Adaption Interview,
     Pregnancy Symptoms Questionaire, State
     Anxiety Scale, Perceived Social Support
     Index. 6) The most effective predictor of
     severe postpartum depression was life
     stress. Interestingly, the longer the
     duration in the U.S., and to some extent a
     greater level of acculturation, were
     related to pregnancy and postpartum
     complications.

600. Tentoni, Stuart C., and Kathleen A. High.
     1980 "Culturally Induced Postpartum
     Depression: A Theoretical Position."
     JOGN. 9(4):246-249.

     1) Prospective. 2) 49 primigravidas,
     18-30 years of age, from middle to upper
     middle socioeconomic and educational
     backgrounds in Milwaukee. 3) Subjects
     were given a 10-item questionnaire before
     attending CEA classes. Follow-up
     interviews were conducted by clinical
     psychologists (no specifics provided). 4)
     see #5. 5) Criteria adapted from Davidson
     1972 and Ruth 1975. 6) Results show three
     distinct theoretical factors emerged which
     are related to a loss of self-esteem and
     these are changes in body proportions,

changes in public attitudes, and changes
in social life. These factors lay the
ground work for depression. 7) This
article suggests that child-birth classes
are psychologically beneficial.

601. Tetlow, C.
1955 "Psychoses of Childbearing." J. MENT.
SCI. 101:629-639.

602. Thomas, C.L., and J.E. Gordon.
1959 "Psychosis After Childbirth:
Etiological Aspects of a Single Impact
Stress." AM. J. MENT. SCI. 238:145-170.

603. Thornton, W.E.
1977 "Folate Deficiency in Puerperal
Psychosis." AM. J. OBSTET. GYNEC.
129:2, 222.

604. Thuwe, Inga.
1974 "Genetic Factors in Puerperal
Psychosis." BR. J. PSYCHIAT.
125:378-385.

1) Retrospective, with good summary. 2)
47 women who had postpartum depression
between 1872-1926; 120 children at least
15 years of age from 43 of the
above-mentioned mothers; 173 grandchildren
at least 15 years of age from 34 of the
above-mentioned grandmothers; and a
control group was selected on a one-to-one
basis with the greatest similarity for
children and grandchildren. 4) Depression
for the initial group of women was defined
as : a) Suffering from their first attack
of the illness and b) Illness originated
within 6 weeks of delivery. 5) Detailed
records of the subjects involved were
obtained through their communities and

psychiatric hospitals and compared with
the controls. They were compared in 11
categories. 6) Statistically significant
differences were found in the child
generation when comparing a) mental
hospital care, b) psychotic reactions
among these, c) total of psychotic
reactions, d) total receiving mental
hospital, clinic, or out-patient care, and
e) total receiving care or suicide and
sick certification out of all subjects.
No significant differences were found in
the generation of grandchildren but there
was a tendency for the numbers to be
greater for the experimental group to
receive care than the control group. This
study provides strong evidence for the
presence of genetic factors in the
category of postpartum depression.

605. Tyndel, M.
1964 "Die Wochenbettdepression.
Deskussionbemerkungen zur Arbeit von
Helmut Luft: 'Die Wochenbettdepression.
Klinik und pathogenetische Faktoren.'
DER NERVENARZT 35(8):366-368.

606. Tod, E.D.M.
1964 "Puerperal Depression. A Prospective
Epidemiological Study." LANCET
2:1264-1266.

607. _____.
1966 "Puerperal Psychoses." BR. MED. J.
5529:1594.

608. _____.
1971 "Puerperal Depression." BR. J.
PSYCHIAT. 119(552):587.

609. Tooley, P.H..
     1965 "Psychiatric and Psychological
     Disturbances of Pregnancy and the
     Puerperium." PRACTITIONER 194:772-780.

610. Treadway, C. Richard; Francis J, Kane,
     Jr.; Ali Jarrahi-Zadeh; and Morris A.
     Lipton.
     1969 "A Psychoendocrine Study of Pregnancy
     and Puerperium." AM. J. PSYCHIAT.
     125(10):1380-1386.

611. Tucker, W.I.
     1962 "Progesterone Treatment in Postpartum
     Schizo-Affective Reactions." J.
     NEUROPSYCHIAT. 125:150-153.

612. Turnbull, J.M.
     1969 "Mental Illness in the Puerperium."
     CANAD. PSYCHIAT. ASSOC. J. 4:525-526.

     1) Historical literature review. 6)
     Author reviews the various etiologies
     offered for puerperal mental illnesses
     dating from the Kahun Papyrus (C.1900 B.C)
     to the turn of the century. Early authors
     followed the hippocratic tradition of
     humours and the notion of milk fever while
     later authors realized there was no form
     of insanity which could not occur in the
     postpartum. Other authors mentioned
     include Esquirol, Clouston, Zilboorg, and
     Freeze, among others.

613. Tylden, E.
     1977 "Psychiatric Disorders Including Drug
     Therapy and Addiction." CLIN. OBSTET.
     GYNAECOL. 4(2):435-449.

614. Uddenberg, Nils.
     1974 "Reproductive Adaptation in Mother
          and Daughter. A Study of Personality
          Development and Adaptation to
          Motherhood." ACTA PSYCHIAT. SCAND.,
          SUPPL. 254.

615. Uddenberg, Nils, and L. Nilsson.
     1975 "The Longitudinal Course of
          Para-Natal Emotional Disturbance."
          ACTA. PSYCHIAT. SCAND. 52(3):160-169.

616. Uddenberg, Nils, and Irmelin Englesson.
     1978 "Prognosis of Post Partum Mental
          Disturbance: A Prospective Study of
          Primiparous Women and Their 4
          1/2-year-old Children." ACTA. PSYCHIAT.
          SCAND. 58(3):201-212.

617. Uddenberg, Nils; Carl Fredrik Fagerstrom;
     and Zaunders Margareta Hakanson.
     1976 "Reproductive Conflicts, Mental
          Symptoms during Pregnancy and Time in
          Labour." J. PSYCHOSOM. RES.
          20(6):575-581.

618. Upreti, Nayantara Sharma.
     1979 "A Study of the Family Support
          System: Child Bearing and Child Rearing
          Rituals in Kathmandu, Nepal." DISS.
          ABSTR. Univ. of Wisconsin, Madison,
          Wis.

1) Ethnographic. 2) Women living in or
near Kathmandu were observed. 6) Author
demonstrates the effectiveness of
childbearing and rearing rituals on the
prevention of physical and emotional
illness in Nepalese women of reproductive
age. No evidence of postpartum depression
was found. Author hypothesizes that the

extended family system and community
support network, expressed through ritual,
allayed this potentially dangerous
postpartum illness.

619. Van Gennep, A.V.
1960 THE RITES OF PASSAGE. Chicago:
University of Chicago Press.

620. Vander Walde, P.; H. Vander Walde; D.
Meeks; and H.U. Grunebaum.
1968 "Joint Admission of Mothers and
Children to a State Hospital." ARCH.
GEN. PSYCHIAT. 18:706-711.

621. Vanputten, R., and J. Lawall.
1981 "Postpartum Psychosis in an Adoptive
Mother and in a Father." PSYCHOSOM. AT.
22(12):1087-1089.

622. Vestal, K.W., and C. McKenzie.
1983 HIGH RISK PERINATAL NURSING.
Philadelphia: W.B. Saunders.

623. Victoroff, V.M.
1952 "Dynamics and Management of
Parapartum Neuropathic Reactions." DIS.
NERV. SYSTEM 13(10):291.

624. Vislie, H.
1956 PUERPERAL MENTAL DISORDERS.
Copenhagen: Munksgaard.

625. Von Hagen, K.
1943 "Mental Illness Following Pregnancy."
CALIFORNIA AND WEST. MED. 58:324-327.

626. Von Kruger, Helmut.
1964 "Die Wochenbettspsychose im Wandel
der Anschauungen." DER NERVENARZT
35:448-458.

627. _____.
1965 "Zur Psychodynamik der
Gestationpsycosen." PSYCHOTER. MED.
PSYCHOL. 15(6):231-252.

628. Von Moschel, Renate.
1956 "Hirnbefund die erner todlich
verlauffenden Wochbettpsychose." DER
NERVENARZT 27:211-215.

629. Wainwright, W.H.
1966 "Fatherhood as a Precipitant of
Mental Illness." AM. J. PSYCHIAT.
123:40-44.

630. Wako, T., and H. Fuji.
1973 "Physiological Management of
Hospitalized Psychiatric Patients."
JAP. J. CLIN. PSYCHIAT. 2:497-503.

631. Walter, S.D.
1977 "Seasonality of Mania: A
Reappraisal." BR. J. PSYCHIAT.
31:345-350.

632. Wayne, G.J.
1952 "Depressive Reactions During
Gestation and the Puerperium." AM. J.
OBST. & GYNEC. 64:1282-1288.

633. Webster, J.
1848 "Remarks on the Statistics,
Pathology, and Treatment of Puerperal
Insanity." LANCET 2:611-612.

634. Weintraub, W.
1978 "Postpartum Reactions." In:
PSYCHIATRIC PROBLEMS IN MEDICAL
PRACTICE. (G. Balis, L. Wurmser, E.
McDaniel, and R. Grenell, eds.) Boston:
Butterworths.

635. Weissman, Myrna M.
     1978 "Sex-Related Factors in Female
     Depression." MED. ASPECTS HUMAN SEX.
     12(3):59-60.

636. _____.
     1980 "Depression." In: WOMEN AND
     PSYCHOTHERAPY. (Annette M. Brodsky and
     Rachel T. Hare-Mustin, eds.) New York:
     The Guilford Press. XVII + 428.

637. Weissman, Myrna M., and Rise Siegel
     1972 "The Depressed Woman and Her
     Rebellious Adolescent." SOCIAL CASEWORK
     53(9):563-570.

638. Weissman, Myrna M., and Eugene S. Paykel.
     1974 THE DEPRESSED WOMAN. A STUDY OF
     SOCIAL RELATIONS. Chicago: University
     of Chicago Press. XX + 289 pp.

639. Weissman, M.M., and G.L. Klerman.
     1977 "Sex Differences and the Epidemiology
     of Depression." ARCH. GEN. PSYCHIAT.
     34:98-111.

640. Wenderlein, J.M.
     1976 "Psychological-Sociological Views on
     S218 (Study of 379 Pregnant Women and
     Women in Puerperium)." ZENTRALBL.
     GYNAEKOL. 98(9):527-532. (Eng. Abs.)

641. Wertz, Richard W., and Dorothy C. Wertz.
     1977 LYING-IN: A HISTORY OF CHILDBIRTH IN
     AMERICA. New York: Schocken Books.

642. Whalley, L.J.; D.F. Roberts; J. Wentzel;
     and A.F. Wright.
     1982 "Genetic Factors in Puerperal
     Affective Psychoses." ACTA. PSYCH. SC.
     65(3):180-193. (Scotland)

643. Whalley, L.J.; I.C. Robinson; and G. Funk.
     1982 "Oxytoxin and Neurophysin in
     Postpartum Mania." LANCET 2(8294):3878.

644. Whelen, E.M.
     1979 "The 'After-Baby Blues.'" AM. BABY
     41(21):16, 20.

645. White, E.W.
     1903 "A Note on the Treatment of Puerperal
     Insanity." BR. MED. J. 1:306.

646. White, M.A., et al.
     1957 "Obstetrician's Role in Postpartum
     Mental Illness." J. AM. MED. ASSOC.
     165:138-143.

647. Wick, S.
     1941 "Puerperal Psychoses." WISCONSIN MED.
     J. 40:299-302.

648. Williams, H.B.
     1938 "Mental and Nervous Diseases
     Associated with Childbirth." MED. J.
     AUST. 2(17):677-681.

649. Williams, J.H.
     1977 PSYCHOLOGY OF WOMEN. New York:
     Norton. Chapter 9, pp. 258-284.

650. Wilson, E.A., and T. Christie.
     1925 "Puerperal Insanity." BR. MED. J.
     II:797-799.

651. Wilson, James E.; Peter Barglow; and
     William Shipman.
     1942 "Prognosis of Postpartum Mental
     Illness." COMPR. PSYCHIATRY 13:305-316.

652. Winokur, George, and Sompop Ruangtrakool.
     1966 "Postpartum Impact on Patients with
     Independently Diagnosed Affective
     Disorder." J. AM. MED. ASSOC.
     197(4):242-246.

653. Winokur, George; Paula J. Clayton; and
     Theodore Reich.
     1969 MANIC DEPRESSIVE ILLNESS. St. Louis:
     C.V. Mosby. VII + 186.

654. Withersty, D.J.
     1977 "Postpartum Emotional Disorders." W.
     VA. MED. J. 73(7):149-150.

655. Yalom, I.D.; D.T Lunde; and R.H. Moos.
     1968 "Post-Partum Blues Syndrome: A
     Description and Related Variables."
     ARCH. GEN. PSYCHIAT. 18:16-27.

     1) Prospective. 2) 39 women who attended
     an Obstetrics Clinic in Palo Alto. 3)
     Mothers were studied one month before
     delivery and for 10 days postpartum. They
     were measured by interviews, behavioral
     observations, and psychological tests. 5)
     4-Point Scale (absent, mild, moderate,
     severe) and a 9-Point Scale (anxiety,
     depression, irritability, distractibility,
     physical appearance, nervousness, sadness,
     fatigue, and sleep disturbances); Nowlis
     Mood Adjective Check List; Porteus Maze
     Test. 6) The following factors are not
     correlated with postpartum depression:
     sex of the child, age of the mother,
     previous mental state, prenatal

complications or kinds of medication.
However, first pregnancy and changing role
expectations are factors related to
postpartum depression.

656. Yarden, P.E., D.M. Max; and Z. Eisenbach.
1966 "The Effect of Childbirth on the
Prognosis of Married Schizophrenic
Women." BR. J. PSYCHIAT. 112:491-499.

657. Yen, R., and N. Quesenberry.
1976 "Pituitary Function in Pseudocyesis."
J. CLINICAL ENDOCRINOLOGY AND METABOLISM
43:132-136.

658. Yorburg, B.
1974 SEXUAL IDENTITY: SEX ROLES AND SOCIAL
CHANGE. New York: Wiley and Sons.

659. Youngs, David, and Mary Lucas.
1980 "Postpartum Depression: Hormonal
versus Alternative Perspectives." In:
PSYCHOSOMATIC OBSTETRICS AND GYNECOLOGY.
New York: Appleton.

1) Summary-commentary. 6) A good general
description of the clinical presentation
of depression. From observation authors
suggest that conflicts focus on the
mothering role, including a sense of
inadequacy, ambivalent or hostile feelings
toward the infant, and fear of injuring
the baby. Regarding prevention and
treatment authors suggest a complete
psychosocial history. While psychotrophic
medication is mentioned authors state "The
primary focus for treating depression
should rest on the identification and
resolution of personal and environmental
stress factors," especially role conflict.

660. Zilboorg, Gregory.
      1928 "Malignant Psychoses Related to
           Childbirth." AM. J. OBSTET. GYNEC.
           15:145-158.

661.   _____.
        1928 "Post-Partum Schizophrenias." J.
             NERV. & MENT. DIS. 68:370-383.

662.   _____.
        1929 "The Dynamics of Schizophrenic
             Reactions Related to Pregnancy and
             Childbirth." AM. J. PSYCHIAT.
             8:733-766.

663.   _____.
        1931 "Depressive Reactions Related to
             Parenthood." AM. J. PSYCHIAT.
             87:927-962.

JOURNAL ABBREVIATIONS

A. Arch. Neurol. & Psychiat.   American Medical
                                             Association Archives of
      Neurology and
      Psychiatry

Abnormal Psychiat.   Abnormal Psychiatry
Actas Luso Esp. Neurol.   Actas Luso Espanolas de
      Neurologia, Psiquiatria y
      Ciencias Afines

Acta Psychiat. Scand.   Acta Psychiatrica
      Scandinavica

Acta Psychotherapy Suppl. Acta Psychotherapy
      Supplementum

Albany M. Ann.   Albany Medical Annuals
Allg. Ztschr. Psychiat.   Allgemeine Zeitschrift fur
      Psychiatrie und
      Psychisch-Gerichtliche
      Medicin

Am. Anthro.   American Anthropologist
Am. Baby   American Baby
Am. J. Clin. Nutr.   American Journal of
      Clinical Nutrition

Am. J. Epid.   American Journal of
      Epidemiology

Am. J. Insan.   American Journal of
      Insanity

Am. J. Nurs.   American Journal of Nursing
Am. J. Obstet. Gynec.   American Journal of
      Obstetrics and
      Gynecology

Am. J. Orthopsychiat.   American Journal of
      Orthopsychiatry

Am. J. Psychiat.	American Journal of Psychiatry
Am. J. Psychotherapy	American Journal of Psychotherapy
Am. J. Public Health	American Journal of Public Health
Am. Med. Assoc. Arch. Gen. Pyschiat.	American Medical Association Archives of General Psychiatry
Am. Med. Quart.	American Medicine Quarterly
Ann. Endocr.	Annales D. Endocrinologie
Ann. Gynec.	Annales de Gynecologie
Ann. Med. Psych.	Annales Medico Psychologiques
Arch. Psych.	Archive fur Psychologie
Arch. F. Gynakol.	Archives fur Gynakologie
Arch. F. Psychiat.	Archives fur Psychiatrie
Archiv. Fur Psychiat. Zeitschrift Neurologic	Archives fur Psychiatrie Zeitschrift Neurologic
Arch. Gen. Psychiat.	Archives of General Psychiatry
Arch. Neurol. Psychiat.	Archives of Psychiatry and Neurological Sciences
Arch. Sex. Behav.	Archives of Sexual Behavior
Aust. NZ J. Psychiatry	Australian and New Zealand Journal of Psychiatry
Aust. Paediatr. J.	Australian Paediatric Journal
Biol. Psychiat.	Biological Psychiatry
Birth Family J.	Birth and the Family Journal
Boston M. & S. J.	Boston Medical and Surgery Journal
Boston Soc. Psychiat.	Boston Society of Psychiatry
BRREA	Brain Research
Bratisl. Lek. Listy	Bratislavske Lekarske Listy
Br. J. Clin. Prac.	British Journal of Clinical Practice
Brit. J. Med. Psychol.	British Journal of Medical Psychology
Br. J. Prev. & Soc. Med.	British Journal of Prevention and Social Medicine

Br. J. Psychiat.	British Journal of Psychiatry
Br. J. Soc. Psychiat. Comm. Health	British Journal of Social Psychiatry
Br. Med. J.	British Medical Journal
Br. Pharmacol. Soc.	British Pharmacological Society
Bull. Acad. Med. Toronto	Bulletin of the Academy of Medicine, Toronto
Bull. Menn. Clin.	Bulletin of the Menninger Clinic
Bull. NY. Acad. Med.	Bulletin of the New York Academy of Medicine
California and West. Med.	California and Western Medicine
Can. J. Public Health	Canadian Journal of Public Health
Canad. Nurse	Canadian Nurse
Canadian Med. Assoc. J.	Canadian Medical Association Journal
Canadian Psychiat. Assoc. J.	Canadian Psychiatrical Association Journal
Child Care Health Dev.	Child Care, Health and Development
Child Psychiat. and Human Dev.	Child Psychiatry and Human Development
CIBA Found. Symp.	CIBA Foundation Symposium
Clin. Endocrinol.	Clinical Endocrinology
Clin. Obstet. Gynaecol	Clinical Obstetrics and Gynaecology
Clin. Psychiat.	Clinical Psychiatry
Clin. Res.	Clinical Research
Compr. Psychiatry	Comprehensive Psychiatry
C. Anthr.	Current Anthropology
Curr. Pract. Obstet. Gynec. Nurs.	Current Practice in Obstetrical and Gynecological Nursing
Curr. Psychiat. Therapy	Current Psychiatric Therapies
Danish Med. Bull.	Danish Medical Bulletin
Dis. Nerv. System	Diseases of the Nervous System

Early Child Dev. Care	Early Child Development and Care
East Afr. Med. J.	East Africa Medical Journal
E. Anthropol.	Eastern Anthropologist
Electroencephalogr. Clin. Neurophysiol.	Electroencephalography and Clinical Neurophysiology
Foren. Psychiatry	Forensic Psychiatry
Fortschr. Neurol. Psychiat.	Fortschritte Der Neurologie-Psychiatrie
Guy's Hosp. Rep.	Guy's Hospital Report
Health Soc. Work	Health and Social Work
Hosp. Comm. Psychiat.	Hospital and Community Psychiatry
Hosp. Commun.	Hospital Community Psychiatry
Human Devel.	Human Development
Human Org.	Human Organization
Illinois M. J.	Illinois Medical Journal
Indian J. Psychiat.	Indian Journal of Psychiatry
Int. J. Behavioral Dev.	International Journal of Behavioral Development
Isr. Ann. Psychiat.	Israel Annals of Psychiatry and Related Disciplines
Ir. J. Med. Sci.	Irish Journal of Medical Science
Isr. Ann. Psy.	Israel Annals of Psychiatry & Related Disciplines
Jahrb. F. Psychiat.	Jahrbucker Fur Psychiatrie
Jap. J. Clin. Psychiat.	Japanese Journal of Clinical Psychiatry
J. Abnormal Psychol.	Journal of Abnormal Psychology
J. Adolescent Health Care	Journal of Adolescent Health Care
J. Affect. Disorders	Journal of Affective Disorders
J. Am. Med. Women's Assoc.	Journal of American Medical Women's Associati
J. of Asthma Research	Journal of Asthma Research

J. Child Psychol. and Psychiat.	Journal of Child Psychology and Psychiatry and Allied Disciplines
J. Child Psychotherapy	Journal of Child Psychotherapy
J. Chron. Dis.	Journal of Chronic Diseases
J. of Clinical Endocrinology and Metabolism	Journal of Clinical Endocrinology and Metabolism
J. Clin. Exper. Psychopath.	Journal of Clinical Experimental Psychopathology
J. Clin. Psych.	Journal of Clinical Psychology
J. Pediatrics	Journal of Pediatrics
J. Personality and Social Psychology	Journal of Personality and Social Psychology
J. Preventive Psychiatry	Journal of Preventive Psychiatry
J. of Psychosomatic Obstetrics and Gynaecology	Journal of Psychosomatic Obstetrics and Gynaecology
J. Ment. Sci.	Journal of Mental Science
J. Nerv. & Ment. Dis.	Journal of Nervous and Mental Disease
J. Neuropsychiat.	Journal of Neuropsychiatry
J. Nurse-Midwifery	Journal of Nurse-Midwifery
JOGN	Journal of Obstetrical and Gyneocological Nursing
J. Obstet. Gynaec. Br. Emp.	Journal of Obstetrics and Gynaecology of the British Empire
J. Psychiat. Res.	Journal of Psychiatric Research
J. Psychosom Res.	Journal of Psychosomatic Research
J. of Reproductive Med.	Journal of Reproductive Medicine
J. Am. Acad. Child Psychiat.	Journal of the American Academy of Child Psychiatry
J. Am. Acad. Psychoanal.	Journal of the American Academy of Psychoanalysis
J. Am. Med. Assoc.	Journal of the American Medical Association

J. Indian Med. Assoc.	Journal of the Indian Medical Association
J. Kansas Med. Soc.	Journal of the Kansas Medical Society
J. M. Soc. New Jersey	Journal of the Medical Society of New Jersey
J. Natl. Med. Assoc.	Journal of the National Medical Association
Matern. Child Nurs. J.	Maternal Child Nursing Journal
M. Bull. Univ. Cal. M. Center	Medical Bulletin, University of California Medical Center
M. Bull. Univ. Southern Cal.	Medical Bulletin, University of Southern California
Med. Hypothesis	Medical Hypothesis
Med. J. Aust.	Medical Journal of Australia
Med. Rec.	Medical Record
Med. Klin.	Medizinische Klinik
Midwives J.	Midwives Journal
Mschr. Psychiat. Neurol	Monatsschrift fur Psychiatrie und Neurologie
Mt. Sinai J. Med.	Mt. Sinai Journal of Medicine
Neuropharm.	Neuropharmacology
New Engl. J. Med.	New England Journal of Medicine
New York State J. Med.	New York State Journal of Medicine
NZ. Med. J.	New Zealand Medical Journal
Nurs. Clin. North Am.	Nurse Clinician of North America
Nurs. Mirror	Nursing Mirror
Nurs. Mirror and Midwives J.	Nursing Mirror and Midwives Journal
Nurs. Outlook	Nursing Outlook
Nurs. Times	Nursing Times
Obstet. Gynecol.	Obstetrics and Gynecology
Postgr. Med.	Postgraduate Medicine

Practition.	Practitioner
Proc. M. Soc. London	Proceedings of the Medical Society of London
Proc. R. Soc. Med.	Proceedings of the Royal Society of Medicine
Prostagland.	Prostaglandius
Psychiat. Clin.	Psychiatria Clinica
Psychiat. Quart.	Psychiatry Quarterly
Psychoanal. Quart.	Psychoanalysis Quarterly
Psychoanal. Study Child	Psychoanalytic Study of the Child
Psych. Bull.	Psychological Bulletin
Psychol. Med.	Psychological Medicine
Psychol. Reports	Psychological Reports
Psychol. Res. Bull.	Psychological Research Bulletin
Psychoneuroendocrin.	Psychoneuroendocrinology
Psychophysl.	Psychophysiology
Psychosom. Med.	Psychosomatic Medicine
Psychosomat.	Psychosomatics
Res. Assn. for Res. in Nerv. Ment. Diseases	Association for Research in Nervous & Mental Diseases
Rev. de Psic. Gral. y Apl.	Revista de Psicologia General y Aplicada
Rev. Med. Intern.	Revista de Medicinia - Interna
Roy. Coll. Gen. Pract.	Royal College of Physicians of London
Schweiz. Med. Wchenschr.	Schweizerische Medizinische Wochenschrift
Silliman J.	Silliman Journal
Social Case.	Social Casework
Soc. Psychiat.	Social Psychiatry
Soc. Res.	Social Research
Soc. Sci. Med.	Social Science and Medicine
Southern Med. J.	Southern Medical Journal
St. Louis M. & S. J.	St. Louis Medical and Surgical Journal
Transactional Anal.	Transactional Analysis
Tr. New Engl. Obstet. & Gynec. Soc.	Transactions of the New England Obstetrical and Gynecological Society
Trop. Geogr. Med.	Tropical and Geographical

W. Va. Med. J.	West Virginia Medical Journal
West. M. Rev.	Western Medical Review
Wisconsin M. J.	Wisconsin Medical Journal
Z. Geburtsch. Gynak.	Zeitschrift fur Geburtshilfe und Gynakologie
Zentralbl. Gynaekol.	Zentralblatt fur Gynaekologie
Zh. Neuropatol. Psikhiatr.	Zhurnal Nevropatologii i Psikhiatrii

SUBJECT INDEX

GEOGRAPHICAL AND CULTURAL INDEX